A Double Life

SIR WILLIAM HAYTER

A Double Life

HAMISH HAMILTON
LONDON

First published in Great Britain 1974
by Hamish Hamilton Ltd
90 Great Russell Street, London WC1

Copyright © 1974 by Sir William Hayter

SBN 241 89040 3

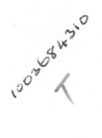

PRINTED IN GREAT BRITAIN
BY EBENEZER BAYLIS AND SON LTD
THE TRINITY PRESS, WORCESTER, AND LONDON

Contents

Prologue   I

1 A BIDDABLE CHILD   5

2 AN OXFORD FAILURE   13

3 A BUDDING DIPLOMAT   19

4 A MARRIED MAN   45

5 A PROMISING CAREER   72

6 A DIFFICULT EMBASSY   98
    i   First Impressions
    ii Soviet Personalities
    iii Soviet Foreign Policy
    iv Khrushchev v. Malenkov
    v   The Twentieth Party Congress
    vi Bulganin and Khrushchev in England
    vii Hungary and Suez

7 AN EARLY RESIGNATION   155

Epilogue   181

For Martha
later on

Prologue

The man next to me fidgeted, scribbled in a notebook, shuffled his feet. At the end of the first movement I said in a polite, just-down-from-Oxford voice, 'Could you possibly make a little less noise?'

'Mind your own bloody business.'

The music started again immediately. The next three movements were played without a break. I had never heard the Ninth Symphony before, and listened absorbed and rather puzzled. My neighbour sat in a tense, rigid silence. At the end, as I got up to go, he was between me and the end of the row.

'I give you the choice of swords or pistols,' he said, 'tomorrow morning at eight.'

Although this was Vienna, where duelling seems a little less absurd than in England, I did not feel obliged to take this very seriously. Besides, he was an Englishman, with a silly toothbrush moustache. 'Don't be ridiculous,' I said, 'I can't use either.' He then told me the story of his life. It cannot have been very interesting, or I must have been very inattentive; I can remember nothing about it.

This apparently pointless anecdote contains two interesting lessons. First, the impulse to tell someone the story of one's life is irresistible, even in the most unpropitious circumstances. Secondly, it is very unlikely that your audience will be interested. If I had then retaliated in kind my own story would probably have been even less memorable. A scholarship and success at Winchester, my father's death, a scholarship and failure at Oxford, an apparently forlorn attempt to get into the Foreign Office; this would have been my simple history. The forlorn attempt, however, later succeeded, and the ensuing years have provided some more interesting material. If you have the kind of career I had in the Diplomatic Service, you inevitably meet important persons. When I retired from the Service in 1958 I could say that besides being fairly intimate with most of the current Politburo, I had lunched with the current Pope (John XXIII, who as Cardinal Roncalli had been Nuncio in Paris when I was there), the current President of the United States (General Eisenhower, European Commander when I was in Paris) and the current President of the French Republic (General de Gaulle, who had invited me as part of Mr. Macmillan's entourage when the latter visited Paris in June 1958); that I had met Chou En-lai (though not Mao Tse-tung) and had dined with the Chiang Kai-sheks in Chungking, and with Sir Winston Churchill at Chartwell; that I had given a party attended by Khrushchev, Nehru and Mrs. Gandhi; that I had been received by the Shah of Iran, the Bey of Tunis, the Kings of Iraq and Jordan, the Ruler of Kuwait and the Sultan of Muscat. Most of this is mere name-dropping; on many of these occasions nothing significant passed, or if it did I did not hear it, and I have already skimmed the cream off my public life, such as it was, by describing my Russian experiences in a book, *The Kremlin and the Embassy*, which I published in 1966. I thought when I wrote that book that it would record all of my career that I should ever wish to record. But the temptation to autobiography is back again, and undeterred by the sad case of my neighbour in the Musikvereinssaal I yield to it. My original intention this time was only to describe those sections of my life that were omitted, or only briefly touched on, in *The Kremlin and the Embassy*. But on reflection it seemed a pity to leave out what was, after all, perhaps the most significant period of my diplomatic career, and so I have incorporated fairly extended sections from my earlier book in this one. If any reader of this new book by any chance recalls passages he encountered in the old one, and feels defrauded, I can only apologize to him—and advise him to skip. In particular, he could omit all of Chapter 6.

When I was writing *The Kremlin and the Embassy* the Foreign Office kindly allowed me to look at the principal despatches I wrote from Moscow when I was Ambassador there from October 1953 to January 1957. This time, I have not sought any help from official sources, and have done no research beyond reading through some sections of my wife's diary. Apart from this I have relied on my now rather selective memory. But I suppose it selects the events in my life which still seem interesting to me; the rest are not likely to seem interesting to anyone else.

ONE

A Biddable Child

I was born in 1906, in Oxford. My father was a barrister turned Egyptian Civil Servant, my mother was the daughter of a country parson. I did not know my father very well. Though we spent all our winters with him in Cairo, Egyptian summers were then thought to be fatal to European children and we were all brought home in the spring, without him; usually he joined us in the late summer. I went to a boarding-school in England when I was eight and was sundered from him by the First World War; he died, aged 55, within a few months of his retirement in 1924, when I was barely eighteen. In spite of this relative remoteness he set the pattern of my whole life. He gave me his own Christian names, arranged that I should follow exactly his educational career, and suggested to me the profession which I subsequently adopted. Many of my views are his, and we were in many ways alike, though he could do some things I cannot (play golf, for instance, and write light verse). On the other hand, I have some tastes he did not share. For instance, he did not care for sight-seeing as much as I do; he was invited to the opening of Tutankhamen's tomb and said he was too busy to go, and when he took us all to visit Paris and Rouen in 1923 I found I already knew more than he did about most of the things we saw. I have always wondered how we should have got on if he had lived longer; on the whole I hope he would have approved of me, though I expect we should have had some disagreements.

My mother was loving, kind, good and so straightforward that she could not tell the simplest social lie. The only thing she was not quite honest about was her age. She was in fact some years older than my father, and produced her first child (me) when she was nearly forty. My sisters followed two and five years later respectively. She never went to school and was almost entirely uneducated. She was aware that all her three children were much cleverer than she was, but she kept their respect as well as their love.

Our early childhood in Egypt has been portrayed, in colours scarcely too glowing, in my sister Priscilla Napier's book *A Late Beginner*, and there is no need to go into all that again. I later looked back on Cairo as a lost heaven, to which I never returned after I started boarding-school. I often dreamed I was back and occasionally begged my parents to let me come, in vain because school holidays were of course much too short for a journey to Cairo in pre-aeroplane days. On one of his English leaves my father, walking with me along the road from Slough, where we were staying with an aunt, towards Windsor, asked me what I meant to be when I grew up. 'A sailor,' I replied manfully (I had then a great faculty for self-deception). My father suggested that as I was invariably sea sick whenever a ship rocked even slightly, this was not a good choice of profession. I then suggested I might follow him into the Egyptian Civil Service. My father replied that by the time I grew up Egypt would have no further need for British civil servants. He then suggested diplomacy; his friends at the Cairo Residency had told him that private means (which of course I shouldn't have) would no longer be necessary, and he thought it an interesting profession. A biddable child, I agreed at once, without having the least idea what diplomacy was. What is more, with one brief aberration, which will be described later, I stuck to this advice until in due course it came to fruition.

Meanwhile there were various preliminary stages to be got through. My father had been a scholar of Winchester and of New College, Oxford, and thought I should follow this course, which I duly did. To get a Winchester scholarship it was necessary to attend an expensive preparatory school. My parents could not well afford this, but did. I was acutely miserable at the school they chose, and wrote pathetic letters to my mother asking to be taken away, a request my parents inevitably refused. The head-master, though an excellent teacher, was a sadist whose ferocious beatings left his victims' backsides lacerated and bleeding. He never beat me, but he despised me because I was hopeless at all games, and his reports on me were mostly sneering in tone. The First World War was now on, all the better assistant masters were in the army, and we were being taught by the dregs of the educational profession, though in this respect things improved a little when the headmaster swallowed his principles and recruited some women teachers.

The most notable of my contemporaries at that school was Brian Howard, a strange, exotic figure who subsequently figured largely, not much disguised, in the novels of Evelyn Waugh. One Good Friday, on a country walk, as we were crossing a stream on a plank bridge, he was seized with a sudden desire to throw me into the water. A brief struggle followed, at the end of which, to my extreme surprise, I saw Brian sitting in the stream-bed, with wide open, astonished eyes. I have no idea how he got there, I had been merely defending myself.

This seems to be the only pleasurable moment that I can recall from my time at this school. Fifty or more years after I left it my wife and I happened to drive past the place and stopped to look over the playing-fields. A wave of intense misery and depression came over me, a backwash of my unhappy time there. It was indeed the unhappiest period of my life, an unhappiness intensified by the fact that for three years the First World War, in particular the danger of German submarines, pinned my parents and my sisters in Egypt. I was left to spend my holidays with a series of aunts, finally coming to rest with a dour little elder sister of my father's, who lived with a kind but ineffectual husband in a tall, narrow, dark house near Lancaster Gate. Her natural asperity was increased by the recent loss of her only son in the war, and she must have found the presence of a glum, unhappy schoolboy for long periods in her house a burden and a nuisance. I think she meant well by me, but she never bothered to show the slightest affection or interest.

The end of the war produced a transformation scene. My family returned from Egypt, and I left that detestable school on winning a scholarship to Winchester. This was a very different kind of place. There were still too many compulsory games for my taste; I was no less incompetent at them, disliked them all intensely (particularly cricket) and resented the time wasted on them. But the attitude towards them was quite different. All the seventy scholars at Winchester are grouped together in College, the original fourteenth-century core of the school, and formed then, as they still do, a highly intellectual society in which athletic success or failure was not of much account. The Winchester scholarship was then one of the most valuable in the country (my education there cost my parents £7 a term) and it attracted a lot of clever boys; John Sparrow was my exact contemporary, Dick Crossman, Richard Wilberforce and William Empson were a year junior to me. Games mattered as little to most of them as to me. My first three years in the school were not all that happy because I was still frightened of everyone. But then I began to alter; I grew five inches in one year and changed from a bun-faced little boy to a tallish, rather aquiline youth, without so far as I can recollect suffering from any of the pangs of adolescence of which so much is now heard. I acquired plenty of self-confidence, moved quite rapidly up the school and in my penultimate year became a prefect and editor of *The Wykehamist*, the school newspaper. Something was apparently still missing, however; C. E. Robinson, perhaps the most intelligent of the many intelligent masters then teaching at Winchester, gazing at me in his form-room one day, said, 'You seem so good in many ways, and yet you lack something. What is it? A sense of humour, perhaps?' He was, I think, only partly right. I did, and do still, rather lack a suitable sense of humour, but the real gap, I suspect, was a more serious one. What I basically lacked was vitality.

It is always supposed nowadays that boys' boarding-schools must be hotbeds of homosexuality. There was a good deal of talk about this in College, as there was on every other subject, but not so far as I was aware much more than talk, though when College, towards the end of my time there, put on a performance of Marlowe's *Dr. Faustus*, there was very little doubt about which member of College ought to play the part of Lechery in the parade of the Seven Deadly Sins. However the authorities decided that this part must be suppressed, and so the parade occurred with Six Deadly Sins only. This was a star-studded production, with Christopher Hawkes as Faustus and Dick Crossman as Mephistopheles; I myself doubled the minor parts of the Evil

Angel and the Cardinal of Lorraine, my first and last appearance on any stage.

My father, who had been knighted in 1923, retired from the Egyptian Civil Service early in 1924, at the age of 55, and came back to England. The whole family spent the Easter holidays in South Devon. During these holidays I finally lost my belief in Christianity (though I retain a kind of affectionate loyalty to the Church of England). This process had been going on for some time, and was brought to a head when two boys we had known well were killed at about this time climbing a cliff near Sidmouth. I found anything so pointless impossible to reconcile with belief in a benevolent and omnipotent God, and so informed my parents, much to their embarrassment. My father was clearly not well, and we gathered he was to have a minor operation as soon as the holidays were over. His recovery from this operation was slow. All that summer term he was in a wheel-chair. At the end of the term I was due to go to an O.T.C. camp at Tidworth. My mother, who was then living in Winchester, suggested I should beg off this on account of my father's illness. I demurred, not because I wanted to go to camp (which I detested) but because I knew I was a possible candidate to become Prefect of Hall (i.e. head boy) for the next year and was nervous of doing anything that might put the authorities against me and so weaken my chances of that. My mother did not press the matter. On the last day of the term Monty Rendall, the Headmaster, who was on the point of retirement, told me I was to be the next Prefect of Hall, and I went off to camp feeling very elated. But after a few days my mother wrote to me saying my father was asking for me and suggesting I should return at once. When I got back to Winchester she told me my father was dying, and a few days later he was dead. He had just been aware that I was going to be Prefect of Hall, a position he had himself held in his time. When he retired from the Egyptian service Field-Marshal Lord Allenby, who as British High Commissioner had been his chief in Cairo, had written to him that 'whatever good has been achieved, during the last 5 years in Egypt, has been in great measure due to you. Your ready co-operation and your wise counsels have been invaluable to me; and to part with you was a sore trial.' Now he

wrote again to my mother that my father's death was 'to me, the
loss of a dear friend. To no man I owe a greater debt of gratitude.
Through all the stormiest days in Egypt, he was a loyal supporter
and a sure guide; on whom I could confidently rely. Mourned
and respected by all who knew him; British and Egyptian; he
leaves a proud record.'

The day after my father's death, my mother asked me to go
round and see Rendall about a funeral service for him in Winchester College Chapel. Rendall was a man for whom I felt fear
rather than respect; my father, who had known him all his life,
did not like him, and I found his Corsican-brigand style unattractive and rather synthetic. When I visited him on that
August morning we quickly sorted out the details about the
funeral service. He then settled down in his armchair and indicated
that I should sit on his lap. Much surprised, I did what I was told,
and he then began to kiss me, his black bristly moustache scratch-
ing my cheek, talking religion all the time. I found the situation,
though not traumatic, very distasteful. I was too afraid of him
to protest (a great boy of eighteen!) and accepted the situation
passively. A day or two later I had to see him again and the same
performance was repeated. Never at any time did he actually say
anything that referred to the way he was behaving; his talk was
all on the highest religious and moral plane.

I never told anyone about this episode. I have often wondered
since whether Rendall made a habit of this kind of conduct or
whether the tensions of his retirement, which had taken place a
few days before, had broken up some long-standing inhibitions.
I am inclined to think that the latter explanation is the more
likely; habitual indulgence in behaviour of this sort would have
been too dangerous for someone in his position. It never recurred
as far as I was concerned. He wrote me a series of letters, in his
elegant, script-like hand, mostly about religion and the proper
attitude to death. These letters did nothing to restore my lost
beliefs. I even once went, with another friend, to stay with him at
Butley Priory, the extraordinary monastic gate-house in Suffolk
to which he had moved on his retirement. By that time he had
lost interest in me, I am glad to say. It was the coldest week-end
I have ever spent, the only occasion in my life on which I have

taken the carpet off the floor and put it on my bed in an attempt to keep warm.

With all his faults Rendall was a man of powerful character. After his retirement to Suffolk he learnt to drive a car, which he did very dangerously. On one occasion he knocked down a policeman on point-duty in Ipswich. Leaning over the side of his car he said to the recumbent officer, 'Get up, my good man, you are not injured and have only yourself to blame.' The policeman shambled to his feet and waved him on.

I passed the summer holidays after my father's death in a kind of sad daze. The whole pattern of my life, indeed of our family life, seemed to have been broken up and distorted. I had counted on him for so much and expected to do so even more. Now we were going to be left without his help and guidance to set us on our various ways, and much poorer. But when I got back to school the clouds lifted. Being Prefect of Hall was curiously elating, and things seemed somehow all to be going my way. I collected various prizes, and the top scholarship to New College in the autumn. I now felt in a strong enough position to avoid any games I didn't want to play, and refused to play cricket at all. It seemed to be a kind of golden age.

Things improved in other ways too. Rendall, whose teaching had always seemed to me overrated, was replaced in Senior Division (though not yet as Headmaster) by Spencer Leeson, whom I thought the best teacher I had yet encountered. Leeson came straight from being a civil servant to teaching Senior Division, and I can still recall the impact, though not alas the content, of his first hour up to books. It was astonishingly stimulating. His stammer was mainly under control until a point at which he began to say, 'The poet B . . . the poet B . . . the poet B . . .' It was quite some time before we learnt whether the poet was Byron, Burns or Browning; if we had known Leeson better we should have known it was certain to be Browning.

Leeson's influence was not confined to teaching. His out of school contacts with his pupils altered many of their lives, and he nearly changed mine fundamentally. I had been sufficiently impressed by the beauty of the College buildings to start reading books on architecture in order to find out more about them. I then became hooked on architecture and could at one time talk about little else, to Spencer Leeson among others. He persuaded me that I ought to give up all idea of diplomacy and become an architect. He introduced me to Hubert Worthington, a delightful man and the architect of some of the worst buildings in Oxford, including the new Library at New College. He also arranged that I should have drawing lessons from Dick Gleadowe, Winchester's extraordinary art master, the only school-master ever to hold the Slade Professorship at Oxford and the designer of the Stalingrad Sword. Both these experiences were disillusioning. The archi- tectural text-books Worthington made me read were repulsive. A few lessons with Gleadowe convinced me that I could not draw and had no creative ideas. It was obvious that I had misinterpreted my sight-seeing proclivities as a desire to become an architect, for which I was clearly unfitted. Moreover it appeared that to be- come an architect I should have to spend seven years, after Oxford, in some kind of apprenticeship, and I could see no reason why my widowed mother should continue to support me for as long as that. I reverted to diplomacy.

In spite of this disillusioning experience my last year at school was one of almost super-charged happiness. Winchester had taught me many things, some more valuable than others. One thing which I acquired, perhaps subconsciously, from it was the habit of attaching myself to an institution, in such a way as to feel an emotional loyalty to it even while recognizing its defi- ciencies. I transferred this habit to the Foreign Office, and later, though not at first, to New College. Even now, when I read the word Winchester anywhere, even in some extraneous context, it gives me a warm feeling.

TWO

An Oxford Failure

New College looked as if it ought to be Winchester all over again, only more so. The Front Quadrangle was an enlarged version of Chamber Court at Winchester. Most of my friends from College at Winchester came on to New College, and there were others, Commoner Wykehamists like Hugh Gaitskell, Douglas Jay and Kenneth Younger, and even a few from other schools, Frank Pakenham (Longford), Edmund Compton, Herbert Hart, John Witt, Goronwy Rees, who were admitted within this charmed Wykehamical circle. But something seemed to have gone wrong. The golden glow that had surrounded my last year at Winchester faded away, and I did not seem to be doing very well.

For one thing, though I did not admit it to myself at the time, I had entirely lost interest in my subject. It was taken for granted that as the senior classical scholar from Winchester, I should be reading Mods and Greats, the full Oxford classical course. These were not particularly well provided for at New College in my time. Mods, the first part, was taught by H. L. Henderson, a very incompetent teacher and a very disagreeable man. Greats philosophy was taught by H. W. B. Joseph, a powerful figure but not interested in non-philosophers like me, and by Alic Smith, later my predecessor as Warden, a great man but not a great tutor. Only Christopher Cox, the ancient historian, was a first-rate teacher. He did succeed in kindling my interest in Greek history, but too late. I had by then failed, by one alpha, to get my First in Mods. I was vivaed for a First in Greats, very unfairly as I thought, by Robin Dundas of Christ Church, who afterwards sent me one of his characteristic post-cards saying, 'There was not much doubt on your papers, and your viva was decisive.' Many years later, when I returned to Oxford as Warden of New College, he asked me to dinner in Christ Church, and then with pleasure read out from his mark-book his comment on my Greats performance: 'Obviously very well taught, probably beyond the limits of his capacity.' This was at least a well-merited tribute to Christopher Cox's teaching.

A backward glance at this unhappy academic experience inspires in me, I am afraid, considerable scepticism about the value of a classical education. After all those years of assiduous application to Latin and Greek, to Roman and Greek civilization, history and literature, I find myself quite unable to read either language for pleasure and without the slightest desire to involve myself further in the two civilizations, which interest me far less than many others I have never studied at all. Of course there is the argument that classical studies provide a form of mental gymnastics of unique value for training the mind. I know of no evidence for this uniqueness, and cannot see why an equally intensive study of, say, Russian and French literature and history might not do just as well; and by the end one could well be reading Russian and French for pleasure.

Anyway, for whatever reason, there I was at the end of my time at Oxford with two second-class degrees, in this as in so much else following my father's example. But my Oxford failures were not only academic, they were also social. Oxford social life was then very competitive. In the part of it that I knew it tended to revolve round a certain category of don, normally unmarried Fellows living in College and entertaining undergraduates, holding a kind of salon. There was no one like that at New College. At Brasenose there was Maurice Platnauer, who had the best food and wine and the most beautiful rooms. Tom Boase, then a Fellow of Hertford, had interesting guests from other worlds. The most brilliant was Maurice Bowra. He was one of my failures. He came once to my rooms, with a crowd of others, but I was never asked to his. Many years later, when we were both heads of Oxford colleges, our relations attained a degree of synthetic cordiality, but we never really liked each other.

However the most important of all these academic salons was that of F. F. Urquhart, the Dean of Balliol, commonly known as Sligger. His relations with Maurice Bowra were bad, perhaps because they were to some extent rivals but also because, basically, they disapproved of each other; otherwise there was no one in Oxford who was not glad of an invitation from Sligger. Every novel written about life in Oxford between 1910 and 1930 contains a portrait of him. The visitors' book at his chalet in Savoy where he had reading-parties is an almost complete list of the successful Oxford undergraduates of those years.

Sligger was not without his defects. He was something of a snob; most of his young friends were Etonians or Wykehamists. His other flaw might seem to some people more important, though I am not sure that it does to me. David Cecil used to say, when we were electing Fellows of New College in the 1960s, 'What this College needs is a good old-fashioned homosexual of the best type.' He meant the kind of bachelor don who would live in College and take an interest in young men that would be rather more than academic, and when he said it I used to think he probably had Sligger in mind. Certainly Sligger's young friends tended to be good-looking (the guests at his chalet were known to the other inhabitants of the mountain as 'les beaux jeunes hommes de M. Urquhart') and when he got one of them alone he would sometimes fondle him in a mild way. Nobody, so far as I know, minded this very much; it seemed a small price to pay for all that he gave in return.

When Sligger died it was found that he had kept every letter, every note, that anyone had ever written to him. These were carefully sorted out and sent to the writers. Many of them must have been of great general interest; I wonder if all the recipients found theirs of such particular interest as I did mine. The packet reached me in Moscow, and it was startling, in those very alien surroundings, to read an invitation to dinner at the Grid ('and never again say I don't try to introduce you to freshmen'—this I think was Goronwy Rees), a gloomy account of some holiday teaching at Winchester ('on the walls hang faded photographs of the Forum, the Campagna and Tivoli: and a large dirty map of Greece: and the beastly little boys are all fidgeting') and juvenile first reactions to Vienna ('the large Imperial inscriptions about the place do make one regret that the War made the world quite so safe for democracy'). I am astonished on re-reading them to find how forthcoming my letters to Sligger are; they are often pert and tiresome but they are intimate, as if I had been his best friend; and yet he was forty years older than me and had hundreds of friends who wrote to him on exactly the same terms as I did. He had a greater capacity for friendship than anyone I have ever known.

But for Sligger, my life at Oxford would have been very flat. I used to sit in my beautiful rooms in the Garden Quadrangle, unable to concentrate on my work, unable to think of any preferable alternative to work, wondering what on earth to do next. I began to get fat, a trouble that has been with me, scarcely held at bay, ever since. I have always tended to eat and drink too much, I dislike exercise and am not good at disciplining myself. Moreover, life at home was no more enlivening than life at Oxford. My mother had, in conjunction with a sister widowed like herself, bought a rather dreary house, a converted eighteenth-century posting-inn on the Bath Road near Newbury. The cousins with whom we were thus obliged to share our lives were not particularly congenial to me (nor I to them, I imagine). The house was not one to which I was keen to invite my friends. I was there as little as possible, but we were now too poor to afford many holidays away. One Christmas vacation my mother managed to produce enough money to enable Priscilla and me to join a large party skiing at Wengen. Almost all the party was of undergraduate age, but one of them was only fifteen, a determined serious child called Iris Hoare who annoyed the rest of the party by skiing better than any of us, and who when not skiing read rather solemn-looking books in a corner. I did not see much of her (the gap between 15 and 20 is very wide) and we did not meet again for many years, but I married her in the end.

However that was still a long way off. Meanwhile, Oxford was coming to an end, and the future was obscure. Looking back on that unsuccessful, rather plump undergraduate I find it hard to recall all his characteristics and views. As I remember, my ideas were vaguely liberal. I thought the League of Nations likely to be an effective deterrent to another war, and believed in disarmament by agreement. My views on home politics were still more un-formed, and what little social conscience I possessed came to life

rather belatedly. Oxford in the thirties was full of social conscience and political activity; both were almost entirely lacking
there in the twenties. The General Strike of 1926 took place towards the end of my first year. Practically the whole University
went off and engaged in strike-breaking, unloading ships, driving
lorries, becoming special constables. This may or may not have
been a good thing to do, but the point is that most of Oxford did
it without stopping to consider whether it was a good thing or
not, by a kind of herd instinct. I myself became a special constable
in Hampstead; most of the time I spent guarding a gate in Regent's
Park, trying to keep a brazier alight and listening to the lions
roaring in the Zoo. The only unpleasantness I witnessed, trouble
in Camden Town when the trams were brought out on the last
day of the strike, inspired nervous excitement rather than thought,
and I resumed my apolitical existence in Oxford when all was over
completely unperturbed.

My social conscience continued to slumber until a ridiculous
incident which took place a year or two later. I was staying with
John Witt's parents at Alfriston; it was bank-holiday, there were
sports on the village green, and Sir Robert insisted on organizing
John and myself, with Dick Crossman and Douglas Jay who were
also staying there, into a tug-of-war team. We were all of us more
or less unathletic, and the opposing teams, mainly young men
from Brighton, had been practising hard all day. We expected to
be ignominiously defeated. On the contrary, hardly had we
touched the rope than our opponents practically fell into our arms.
Sir Robert reduced our team, enlarged theirs, but nothing we
could do enabled us to lose plausibly. Eventually we shambled
back into the Old Clergy House, feeling that Sir Robert's well-
meant attempt to create good-will hadn't really worked out quite
right.

My family had always regarded itself as poor; almost all my
friends had more money than I had; but this incident made it
clear to me at last that if a dividing line were drawn between rich
and poor, privileged and under-privileged, I was definitely above
it. I and most of my friends had after all always lived in houses
with at least one bathroom and at least two servants, and had
eaten meat at least twice a day; and as a result of this our physique

was automatically superior to that of the large majority of our fellow-countrymen. I had sometimes complacently thought that, given my knack for passing examinations, I should have got just as far if my father had been a labourer as I had as the son of a distinguished Civil servant; I then began to wonder if the meat-meals and the sanitation, the leisure and the room-space, had not had rather more to do with it than I had suspected.

THREE

A Budding Diplomat

About the last thing that happened to me at Oxford was that I got a Laming Travelling Fellowship at Queen's. This enabled, and indeed obliged, me to spend nine months abroad learning languages. French and German were then compulsory subjects for the Foreign Office entrance examination; I had studied both for many years at Winchester and at the end knew practically nothing of either, I could not even decline *der, die, das.* Winchester then taught most subjects well, but modern languages very incompetently. My French had improved a little since then because I have, as it happens, a number of French cousins who live in dilapidated little chateaux near Nantes, and I had spent some months staying with them during university vacations. This was a curiously remote world. Rent was paid in kind; when an apple-tree was picked, half the apples went to the peasant and half to my cousins, the landlords, and when the vintage came the wine, a good Muscadet, went into alternate barrels. Social life was limited; occasionally the only horse on the farm was taken away from the plough and harnessed to a char-à-banc, and we would drive off to call on a neighbouring *propriétaire,* where we would sit drinking grenadine on a dusty, weedy terrace in front of the chateau. There was a muddy little pond in the park, where my cousins would sit for hours fishing for muddy little fish. Nobody spoke a word of English, and I soon became fairly fluent in French and began to read the simpler French novels with enjoyment; I discovered with amused pleasure how much *Les Trois Mous-quetaires,* which I had already read in English, had been bowdlerized in the Everyman translation. It was during one of these visits that I was more completely put down than I ever remember being before or since. One of my cousins was telling me how badly

Englishwomen dressed. I didn't feel this was a topic on which I stood much chance of doing well, so I rather feebly replied that at least Englishmen dressed better than Frenchmen. 'Oui, c'est vrai,' she replied, 'la coquetterie mâle est tres peu developpée en France.' One of my more elderly cousins used to puzzle me by talking, in 1927, about 'l'année de la guerre'; surely the First World War had lasted longer than that? But then I discovered he meant the war of 1870, in which he had fought after having previously guarded the Vatican as a 'Zouave du Pape'.

As my French had thus become distinctly better than my German, I decided to give six of my nine months to the latter. I spent them in Vienna, where the incident described in the Prologue took place. Then I moved to Paris and entered M. Martin's establishment in the rue Madame, so graphically represented in Terence Rattigan's first play *French Without Tears*. One day when I was there Robin Hankey, then a secretary at the Embassy, appeared and asked if any of us had a white tie. I said I had, whereupon he ordered me to dine at the Embassy that evening; there was a party to celebrate the wedding of the Ambassador's daughter and they were short of men. Thrilled at this but terrified, I dressed early, and being afraid of arriving late hurried down to find a taxi. They were rare in that quarter but that evening one appeared immediately, drove me in a flash to the Embassy and deposited me in the courtyard before I could stop him, three-quarters of an hour early. I hung about, anxiously fingering my tie, until the Ambassadress, Lady Tyrrell, appeared. I now thought I should be all right since I knew she was Sligger's sister and we should have a common topic, but she seemed never to have heard of him (she was notoriously vague; on one occasion, mounting the staircase of the Polish Embassy with the Counsellor's wife, she said to the latter, 'Where are we? And who am I?'). My embarrassment increased. No one who subsequently arrived was known to me, my presence appeared inexplicable, and my first introduction to diplomatic life was a disappointing one.

Undeterred, I ploughed on with my preparations. I came back to Oxford in the summer to brush up my Latin composition, in which for some reason I was to be examined for the Foreign Office, and spent a few weeks living in Queen's as a member of that luxuriously beautiful Senior Common Room. My room overlooked the Provost's garden, and from my window I saw that rare spectacle, Provost Magrath. He was the last of the Heads of Houses with life tenure. He was then over ninety, had long ceased to function as the effective head of the college and had outlived a succession of Pro-Provosts who had governed Queen's without being able to move into the Lodgings. Malicious rumour maintained that he had in fact died many years before but that his daughters, unwilling to move out, had replaced him with a stuffed dummy which they manipulated to suggest a semblance of life. I must say that nothing I saw from my window that summer of 1930, of a black-straw-hatted figure surrounded by solicitous female attendants, was necessarily in contradiction with that rumour.

A few weeks later I sat for the Foreign Office examination. For various reasons it was the first and last time I could compete. No one except my mother believed me likely to get in. It was a chilling thought, as we sat scribbling in those hot rooms in Burlington Gardens, distracted by Atkinson's detestable carillon which played idiotic tunes every hour, that the whole future course of our lives depended on scribbling correctly, on answering satisfactorily those endless, searching questions on subjects of which most of us knew so little. But I was lucky in the questions; I scribbled, it seems, correctly, and after an interminable wait found that I had passed in third, two places behind Frank Roberts and one ahead of Duncan Sandys.

This was, in fact, how one got into the Diplomatic Service in those days. One took a competitive examination which, with the addition of a few extra compulsory subjects, was identical with that for the Home Civil Service. But no one believed this. There was a widespread illusion that the Service was reserved for persons with political influence and large private means. I possessed neither, nor did the majority of my contemporaries in the Foreign Office. But the illusion persisted that entry to the Service was restricted to rich and privileged aristocrats. There were two main reasons for this persistence. In the first place the senior, and therefore more conspicuous, members of the service were selected under an earlier and since discarded system. In the second place even under the system then current the majority of the entrants came from a few of the major public schools. But the blame for this lay not with the Foreign Office but with the English educational system. To pass a difficult competitive examination a certain educational standard is necessary, and these schools then provided the best means of attaining that standard. Moreover they were attended by the scions not only of the aristocracy but of the upper-middle, or professional, class, and the majority of recent entrants into the Foreign Office belonged, as I did, to the second category. There were very few titles or historic names among the junior members of the service at that time; unfortunately few, perhaps, since titles and historic names were still distinct assets at a number of diplomatic posts, more particularly the republican ones.

I began my diplomatic career at the Foreign Office, where I spent a year in the League of Nations and Western Department, dealing with the affairs of Belgium, Holland and Luxembourg, countries which I had never visited and of which I knew nothing. Spain was also included in the affairs of our Department, and one summer evening, taking a long-distance telephone call from Madrid, I could hear over the wire the shouting of crowds in the streets round the Embassy and was told that Alfonso XIII had abdicated. In September 1931 I was transferred to Vienna. On the way there I went to Geneva as a member of the delegation to the League of Nations Assembly. The delegation should have been headed by Mr. Arthur Henderson, then Foreign Secretary, but a few days before we set out the Labour Government fell and we got instead Lord Cecil, Lord Lytton, Lord Astor and Sir Arthur Salter, who all seemed impressive at the time but who look a little ill-assorted from this distance. I sat behind Sir Arthur Salter in various committees, and handed him draft speeches prepared by more expert hands than mine. The most momentous was one explaining why the pound, which the National Government was formed to save, had nevertheless parted company with the gold standard. This seemed to us all then to bear a very close resemblance to the end of the world. I had, that summer, acted as the most junior secretary of a conference at the Foreign Office attended by the Foreign and Finance Ministers of Great Britain, America, France, Germany and Italy. Ramsay MacDonald had eloquently presided; the object of the Conference had been, so far as I recollect, to save the Mark, and the Prime Minister had used with aplomb the phrase 'as safe as the Bank of England'. M. Laval had leered above his dirty white tie; Dr. Brüning and Colonel Stimson had been precise and factual; Mr. Mellon and M. Briand, tired old men with only a few years to live, had slumbered. I had suffered throughout the Conference from the fact that whereas everyone else was sub-fusc I had only a purplish-brown suit which made me, I felt, distressingly conspicuous. At the end there was a Buckingham Palace Garden party; at this I could at last appear correctly dressed; the sunshine was brilliant, the crowd was large and well-fed in appearance, the Royal Family imposing, and any idea that, as then began to be whispered, the pound could be in danger had seemed absurd. And now, a few weeks later, Geneva shop-keepers were refusing to exchange sterling and distinguished economists were obliged to make embarrassed explanations before committees of sceptical and unimpressed foreigners. But that night I saw Grock for the first time, and the approaching end of the world seemed to matter less.

Shortly before the session ended Geneva received the news of the Mukden Incident. The League at that time was in full strength; only two great Powers, Russia and America were not members, and those two at that time were not yet regarded as super-Powers and were remarkably inactive outside their own borders. It scarcely seemed probable that so apparently solid an institution could be seriously affected by so seemingly remote an occurrence; everyone was in a hurry to get home, the Salle Vitrée was stuffy, and the inarticulate Mr. Yoshizawa, the eloquent Dr. W. W. Yen, were listened to with equal irritation. Closer attention would have detected in the undertones of their controversy the subdued death-knell of the League.

Vienna, which I reached in the autumn of 1931, I found very enjoyable. It provided me with all the pleasures I hoped for in my new career, and more besides. In my oral examination by the Civil Service Commissioners I was asked why I wanted to get into the Foreign Office. I had not expected this question, and mumbled confusedly that my family had always been keen on the idea. This was of course true, but it was not the only reason. More fundamental was my passion for sightseeing. I was too poor ever to be able to travel extensively at my own expense, and my only hope seemed to be to do so at that of the tax-payer. In Vienna my sightseeing proclivities received full satisfaction, and for the first time I learnt to enjoy Baroque. I also advanced my musical education; in the two and a half years I was at the Legation I heard all Beethoven's symphonies, all Mozart's and Wagner's operas, and attended eight performances of *Fidelio* and five of *Rosenkavalier* (I used to go whenever Lotte Lehmann sang Leonora or the Marschallin, and generally this meant a bonus of Elizabeth Schumann as Marzellina or Sophie, and of Richard Mayr as Rocco or Ochs). On the whole I think this was the most profitable thing I did in Vienna; otherwise I wasted my time. The people it would have been interesting to see and know in Vienna were the intellectuals, the musicians, the socialists of the municipality. Unfortunately a juvenile snobbery led me to concentrate on the 'erste Gesellschaft'. Vienna, impoverished as it was, supported in those days two more or less idle societies. The 'erste Gesellschaft', composed largely of Princes and Counts, was a survival of the Court society of pre-war days, for whom the Palais Rothschild had taken the place of the Hofburg as the centre of social life; the 'zweite Gesellschaft', mainly Barons and vons, represented the pre-war bureaucracy and was pro-Nazi because the 'erste Gesellschaft' was anti-Nazi. The two societies disliked each other intensely. I went once with Paukerl Wurmbrand, a Count and very much a member of the 'erste Gesellschaft', to a restaurant where he was not known. The head-waiter addressed him as 'Herr Baron'. 'Don't call me that,' he said sharply, 'call me anything you like, Herr Sanitätsinspektor, Comrade, anything. *Nur nicht Herr Baron.*'

In spite of their occasional absurdities, the members of the 'erste Gesellschaft' were immensely agreeable to know. But they were of no political importance, and had very little to contribute except an easy way of life which they managed to maintain on, in most cases, negligible incomes. There were tea-parties which lasted until it was time to go to bed; and there were little night-clubs where everyone knew everyone else, and drank local wine or beer and danced to very good three-man bands; and most people enjoyed music in an amateurish way; and someone had once met an actor from the Burgtheater. In the summer they all left for dilapidated country houses in Styria or Moravia, full of unsuspected uncles in green-and-grey Jägeranzüge and plain nieces in Dirndls. It was pleasant and entirely pointless, and quite irrelevant to the important issues that were then being fought out in Austria.

The essential issue was, of course, whether Austria could preserve its independence. Few Austrians then really believed it could, and until the Nazi take-over in Germany every Austrian political party favoured the Anschluss, the absorption of Austria into Germany, in greater or lesser degree. When the Nazis came to power in Berlin there was less enthusiasm for the Anschluss, but unfortunately the two parties most opposed to it, the Christian Democrats and the Socialists, were also violently opposed to each other, and the former were drawing closer all the time to the indigenous Fascists, the Heimwehr, to whom the Socialists were anathema. British policy was, theoretically, to support Austrian independence, but there was little that we could do about it, and we were not particularly well-equipped to do it locally. The Legation staff was tiny. When the Minister went on leave the only archivist went on leave too, taking with him his wife who was the Legation's only typist. The entire staff (apart from the porters who were mostly Austrian spies) then consisted for several months of the First Secretary, who became the Chargé d'Affaires, and the Third Secretary (myself). The First Secretary could type, and had to, since I couldn't; but I kept the files and the accounts, did all the ciphering, changed the combination of the safe and did all the other dog's body work. When I visited Vienna after the last war the Embassy there had a staff of over a hundred. I confess I am doubtful whether a staff of that size would have made the slightest difference to Austria's inter-war slide into Germany's arms, and I sometimes wonder what they all do; even with our tiny inter-war staff we were not overworked, and in the summer we seldom came to the office in the afternoon.

But the seriousness of the position in Austria came vividly home to me a few months before I finally left Vienna. One

February morning in 1934 I went with the Minister to the celebration of, I think, a Papal jubilee in St. Stephen's Cathedral. The rich gloom of that murky choir was dispelled by a blaze of electric lights. Half-way through the service these lights faded gradually and went out, leaving Cardinal Innitzer silhouetted against the flames of twenty tall candles on the altar. As we came out through the vestry someone, the Swiss Minister perhaps, said he had heard there had been rioting in Linz that morning. This surprised no one; the Nazis, then, were always rioting in Linz. The odd part of the story was that the rioters were said to have been socialists. Driving back to the Legation we noticed that all the trams had stopped. On arrival we were told that the Socialists had risen and called a general strike.

Even at the first hearing, delivered with the full authority of the Austrian Government, this struck me as a very improbable story. The Socialist municipality of Vienna was one of the most conservative and firmly entrenched institutions in Europe; it had created a magnificent system of social security, and built great blocks of workmen's flats which were the admiration of architects no less than of social workers. The municipality was in an uneasy relationship with the Catholic fascists who by then controlled the Federal Government, but it seemed inconceivable that it should have declared war on them. And so it was. Nothing of the sort. On the contrary, the Federal Government had made an utterly unprovoked attack on the Municipality. All that day and the next we could hear from the Legation the heavy thud of the Government's artillery, pounding on the workmen's flats that all Europe had admired. It was not only a crime, it was a blunder; the Dollfuss party, in destroying the Socialists, destroyed their only effective allies against the Nazis and prepared their own destruction at the hands of Hitler. My landlord, who had Nazi leanings, was delighted. 'The Heimwehr,' he said, 'are doing our dirty work for us.' Though all my friends were fighting with the Heimwehr, I myself was never for a moment in doubt where the right lay.

For the first two days of the fighting I was too busy to leave the Legation, except to walk home through darkened streets to my flat. The aspect of a great city in total darkness has since become familiar enough; then it was an unusual sight to see the stars above the black canyons of the streets. I had to cross the Ring to get to my flat; the Innere Stadt within the Ring contained all the Government offices and was defended by thick barricades of barbed wire, with Heimwehr sentries at the gaps who made the same fuss every time I passed; weeping old women, worried Jews, were pushed around and denied admission. On the third day I had a little leisure, and drove in my car round the outer boulevards where most of the workmen's flats were. As I came down towards the Karl Marx Hof, the largest and handsomest of them, a line of troops with fixed bayonets moved up the road towards me, shepherding a small and orderly crowd in front of them. I expected to be stopped, but they opened and let me through. The Karl Marx Hof appeared deserted, with a gaping shell-hole over one of its arches. I drove under the arch and along behind. Nothing happened. Some friends who next day drove under the same arch were received with a hail of machine-gun bullets. This was the first of several occasions on which I have noticed that my presence has a kind of halcyon effect on armed conflict; I have been through two civil and three international wars, and have yet to see a shot fired in anger.

A few weeks later I heard I was to be transferred to Moscow. I left Vienna in April 1934; in those days there was a through train from Warsaw via Vienna to Cannes; my sister Priscilla was by then married to a naval officer, Trevy Napier, whose ship was at St. Raphael, and I was to spend a few days on the Riviera with them before going on to London and Moscow. I was sorry to leave what was in many ways the perfect post, but I was thrilled with the idea of Moscow and felt I had really had about enough of Vienna. A few weeks before leaving I had, in the company of a visiting M.P., called on Seitz, the Socialist ex-Mayor of Vienna, in his prison; he had received us in his cell with complete dignity and poise, apologizing for its smallness, but this final incident had disgusted me a little with the company I had been keeping in Vienna. However, all my friends appeared at the station to see me off; I had what used to be known in diplomatic circles as 'une bonne gare'; and as my train—really mine, there were no other passengers and I had two sleeping cars and a restaurant-car entirely

to myself—rolled through the pleasant Carinthian villages I reflected that if the 'erst Gesellschaft' had done nothing else for me it
had at least finally cured me of social inferiority complexes.

Soon after my return to England I went to stay with the Clive
Wigrams. He was then Private Secretary to King George V and
lived in the Norman Tower of Windsor Castle. On the morning
I was due to leave them a slightly flustered housemaid informed
us that the King and Queen were coming up the garden. They
shortly entered, accompanied by the Duke and Duchess of York
and Princess Elizabeth (I don't suppose ordinary mortals often
meet two Kings and three Queens of England simultaneously).
I was presented as a young man about to proceed to the Moscow
Embassy. The King turned his penetrating dark-blue stare on to
me. 'They tell me that if one could only get rid of that fellow
Stalin everything would be all right there,' he said (he had some
ex-Grand Duchess living in Windsor Great Park, who used to
feed him misleading émigré rumours). I felt like a courtier of
Henry II—'who will rid me of this troublesome commissar?'—
but was never then or later tempted to act accordingly. Queen
Mary, more practically, asked in her deep voice if I should get
enough to eat. I have no recollection of having received from any
other high authority any more useful comments or guidance on
what I should do or expect when I got to Moscow.

One of my relations, on hearing that I was going to Moscow,
said that it seemed the ideal post for me, 'music, architecture and
no food' (the last reflecting my family's concern about my figure).
Other people took a gloomier view; the isolation in which
foreigners lived in the Soviet Union, and the crowded quarters
in the Embassy, had produced a tendency to despondency in some
of my predecessors. I was more optimistic; the anxieties about the
food supply, though repeated by Queen Mary, proved unfounded,
and in fact I grew much fatter in Moscow. The music, the architecture were there; and there were other interests. For the first
time I was fully able to gratify that passion for tourism which had
largely induced me to enter the Foreign Office.

I travelled out to Moscow with the Chilstons. At the frontier
station the Ambassador ordered caviar and vodka; I followed his
example and sampled for the first time one of the most perfect of

gastronomic combinations. Negoreloe had other points of interest; the famous Russian smell, the tubular frescoes, the meticulous customs officials. After half-an-hour in that station I knew more about the Soviet Union than I had gathered from all the numerous books I had read about it. I had always wanted to go there; I had meant to use the unexpired half of my Laming Fellowship on learning Russian; I was full of curiosity about the régime, and arrived with that famous 'open mind' which usually withers so soon under the impact of Russia's marked personality, to be replaced by abhorrence or devotion.

The British Embassy when I got there seems to have been an odd place. As I wrote to my sister Alethea a few weeks after my arrival, 'virtually everyone in the Embassy, except for the ones who have wives here, is living in sin, which makes considerable complications as we all live in one building: moreover, one or two of them have now married the wenches, which of course makes things more, not less, complicated. The place is consequently full of Russian females of somewhat ill-defined social standing, none of them on speaking terms with the others; meanwhile their "husbands" mostly have wives and families in England to whom they are apt to refer with tears in their eyes after a drink or two (they are most of them pretty perpetually "after a drink or two"). However we are all very hearty, British and middle-class, talk a good deal about cricket, play a good deal of bridge, and in short no one, I mean the casual observer, would know there was anything wrong. Actually of course the people in question are the male typists and so on: the diplomatic side is, so far, pure, though the Translator, who ranks as Third Secretary and has married a fat little Russian after living with her for a year, informed me on my second day that the only way I could hope to keep sane in Moscow was to acquire a Russian girl friend early (he has introduced me to one or two young ladies who I suspect may be candidates for the part).'

This translator left us a few months later. I described his departure in another letter to Alethea. 'There was a touching scene on the platform: all his ex-girl friends, a large tribe, came and wept on his shoulder: what's more, he kissed the Counsellor of the Polish Embassy on both cheeks. His wife, a nice little Russian who's been put through it by the Ogpu, was carrying an immense bouquet and beaming with joy at the idea of getting out of Russia. They'd meant to go the night before: but half an hour before the train left they decided not to, for some reason I never fully understood, and instead came to my room and drank whisky (*faute de* vodka) and generally behaved in a thoroughly Dostoievski manner, breaking several glasses, repeatedly bursting into tears, and telling me long and very interesting stories about the Revolution. He had his faults, but I prefer him to his successor, a well-meaning young man with projecting teeth, a loud voice and a habit of teaching his grandmothers (if I may so describe the Ambassador and myself) to suck eggs. He has already bought two ikons, a thing I have sworn to myself never to do.'

An even more Dostoievskian experience took place during a visit to Leningrad, which I described to Alethea as 'a good town, a real capital, instead of an overgrown village like this place'. There I had a remarkable guide, who told me the story of her life: 'At fourteen she tried to poison herself. At fifteen she tried to shoot herself. At eighteen she ran away from home because her mother wanted her to learn English and she wanted to learn Portuguese: she went to live with an old lady who taught her English: this didn't last long because the old lady objected to her receiving friends in bed, so she got married. Though they hadn't enough to eat, she constantly bought books: at last she had so many that one day when her husband wanted his lunch there was nowhere for him to eat it off except the window-sill, to which she accordingly directed him. The worm turned—he put his plate down on one of her books, and she divorced him. She took up with another man, and had a child: when the child died she married the father: she didn't want to before because if she had the child would have had to bear his name, which is an aristocratic one and therefore a grave disadvantage in this country. But not long after a friend of hers was arrested for the crime of which Röhm and his gentlemen friends were accused: I should say he was guilty, to judge from his picture and the fact that he was friendly with a man at the German Embassy here whose tendencies in that direction were notorious. But to save him she divorced her husband and told the authorities she was the mistress of the man they arrested and wanted to marry him, thinking this would disprove the charge against him. Her husband helped because he and the other man were both intellectuals. But all was in vain and he was sent to Siberia: he is now dead, though she doesn't know it, and she is still living with her divorced husband (though she has not married him and is not faithful to him) in a room about the size of Hamer's bedroom at B.H. [i.e. about eight foot square], but containing a grand piano and an immense quantity of books and several ancestral portraits belonging to various husbands and herself. She supports her ex-husband by guiding various foreigners round Leningrad, including among others Bernard Shaw (she showed me a book autographed by him), Lady Astor and Lady Chilston: in order to be allowed to do so she has to report to the Ogpu on their views, tastes and private lives, with special attention to their vices if any. She speaks seven languages.'

Apart from occasional glimpses of this kind, I was, like all diplomats, almost totally detached from the Russian scene. This detachment was a curious phenomenon. When I first arrived a few of the livelier bachelors at the German Embassy used to entertain quite a number of Russians, chiefly at their *dachas* outside Moscow. As Hitler's anti-Bolshevik tirades grew more intense even this ceased, and from then on the diplomatic corps was reduced to its own company, varied only by rather formal relations with its official Soviet contacts and by exchanges with the foreign correspondents, who were not less isolated than the diplomats. This confinement to diplomatic society was something new to me; in Vienna, except for a few Italian and Hungarian secretaries who went out in the 'erste Gesellschaft', I had known none of my colleagues. There was a tiresome habit there, when a secretary left for another post, of dunning the members of other Legations for a parting present. I had contributed my ten *Schillinge* three or four times a year, and when I left I got my reward, in the shape of an elegant little cigarette case. I do not smoke, and even if I did the case would have been useless since it was too narrow to hold more than three cigarettes. Inside were ten facsimile signatures; four or five I recognized as those of men I had met at some of the larger parties at the British Legation; the rest were completely unknown to me. In Moscow however all the

Secretaries of all the Embassies knew each other, if not intimately,
at least as well as they could bear. There were endless dinner-
parties, indistinguishable from diplomatic dinner-parties elsewhere except that there was an invariable extra course of caviar
and vodka; there was a curiosity-shop called the 'Diplomats'
Club', where the newly arrived colleagues bought ikons and the
old hands Meissen china and English clocks; and there was a con-
tinual exchange, in bad French, of inaccurate political information,
mostly picked up from servants. Their background, and a sub-
conscious resentment of the way in which they were held at arms'
length by the régime, made most of the diplomats anti-Soviet.
Few of them ever left Moscow, except perhaps to go to Leningrad
to see the pictures at the Hermitage, and they all agreed in believing travel in Russia to be uncomfortable to the point of impossibility, and unprofitable even if possible. During the three years
I was there I went twice to Leningrad, three times to the Crimea,
twice to the Caucasus, once to the Ukraine and once down the
Volga, besides many shorter excursions: many of my colleagues
had been there ten years or more, and assured me as I got back
from each of my journeys that to travel in Russia was out of the
question. The unalloyed company of these amiable absurdities
would have been, in the long run, intolerable, but for the fact
that the members of our own Embassy were of an entirely different calibre, and for the presence, here and there in the corps,
and particularly in the German and American Embassies, of
people whose views on the Soviet Union were of real interest.
The journalists, too, were a distraction; they were generally,
owing to their more exposed positions, more cautious than the
diplomats in their expressions about the régime, but their precon-
ceptions were less strong and their reactions generally more
authentic. Then there were the tourists. They were much encouraged in those years, as bringing foreign exchange. There had
always been a steady trickle of pilgrims to the Red Shrines; and
these, in the summers particularly of 1935 and 1936, were surprisingly augmented by most of the former clientele of Salzburg
whom the increasing totalitarianism of Central Europe had driven
to find distraction elsewhere. There were Dramatic Festivals, and
a Persian exhibition; the Gilbert Millars, the Kenneth Clarks,

Claire Luce were staying at the Metropole; I gave a cocktail party for fifty people, not a Russian among them.

The theatre was certainly worth coming for. Lord Chilston was no theatre-goer, but the Ambassadress loved it and I used often to go with her. She knew all the actors and sketched their costumes when they interested her. The Moscow Arts Theatre was then undoubtedly the best in the world. A few days after my arrival in Moscow I saw them act the *Cherry Orchard*; Olga Knipper, Chekhov's widow, took the part of Ranevskaya; I then knew no Russian, but I had a sense of absorption into reality in watching that play which I have never had in any other theatre, English or French, Austrian or American (this absorption of the spectator or reader is, it seems to me, characteristic of Russian literature; when I first read *War and Peace* I had a feeling that I was leading a double life, and that Tolstoy's world was more real than my own). The Bolshoi was musically inferior to the Vienna Opera; but some of its productions of Russian opera were superb, and the ballet, on academic and pre-Diaghilev lines, remained magnificent.

Travel, however, was still the best of all. Uncomfortable though it sometimes is, there is no travel like Russian travel. Old towns like Novgorod and Rostov Veliki, little white churches with gold domes, on tufted green hills by wide lakes; the Volga, in a steamer with a rhythmic vibration suggesting the cygnets' dance in *Swan Lake*, a placid, immense stream, the European bank a cliff, the Asiatic bank a swamp, Kazan, Samara, Stalingrad gleaming on their little hills; the Crimea, a grander, less sophisticated Riviera, where you drove from Sevastopol across the arid uplands of Inkerman and Balaklava until, through the Baidar Gates, you saw the Black Sea four thousand feet down through groves of olive and beech. Best of all the Caucasus, which to me is the most romantically beautiful region on the earth.

Baedeker seems to have found it less romantic. I had recently bought a 1914 edition, from which I quoted, with interjections, in a letter to Alethea just before my first visit there: 'bears are frequently met in the Caucasus, and tigers and panthers occur in the district of Lenkoran. *Venomous serpents* [his italics] are found chiefly in the plains . . . Wounds from the tarantula are rare . . .

Travellers who quit the beaten track should be provided with rugs, a lantern, an air-cushion, rubber overshoes, an alarm-clock [why?], pins and needles, thread, string, straps, preserved meat, condensed milk, bread (seldom obtainable in the mountains and never good), . . . insect powder, wrapping-paper and writing materials . . . There are no *Club Huts* or *Refuges* in the Caucasus . . . Wine should be renounced and tea taken instead [come, come] . . . *Public Safety* is on a somewhat unstable footing'. These, I told Alethea, 'are only a few of his gems: the work must, as second-rate reviewers say, be read in its entirety. Italics are all his: it's awful about the *Club Huts* and the *Venomous Serpents*. Exit,' I concluded, 'pursued by a bear'.

Undeterred by all this, I went twice to the Caucasus in those years. The first time, with Noel Charles, then Counsellor at the Embassy, was in the early summer of 1935. We went by train to Baku via Tiflis, crossed the Georgia Military Highway twice, visited Erivan and came back via the Crimea. The second time, in the autumn of the following year, I covered much the same ground, with excursions into Ossetia, in the company of the German Ambassador, Count Schulenburg, who was subsequently executed for his part in the plot against Hitler. He was a most likeable man, and it is probably just as well that an early divorce made it, in those days, impossible for him ever to be appointed Ambassador in London; he would have repeated, with results no less finally disastrous, the success enjoyed by Prince Lichnowsky in the years before 1914. To travel with in the Caucasus he was perfect. He had been Consul-General in Tiflis during the last war, and produced fascinating stories about shooting wild sheep with Georgian Princes, and German plans for the invasion of India in 1918, 'which events elsewhere unfortunately rendered Utopian'. With him were his daughter and also Johnny Herwarth, who was to be German Ambassador in London after the war, and his wife.

Travelling with an Ambassador had the advantage that we had a heavy Ogpu escort who were invaluable in procuring us transport and accommodation. These serious young men, impeccably dressed in blue serge suits, accompanied us through the wildest regions of the Caucasus, studiously ignoring and ignored. Johnny used to have surreptitious morning colloquies with them explaining our plans; but whenever possible they rode in separate vehicles, and even when circumstances forced us to share the same small char-à-bancs they pretended not to be there.

Count Schulenburg was indeed very kind to me. During our journeyings through the Caucasus I mentioned to him that, much as I appreciated all the caviar one got in Russia, I did miss oysters, of which I had never had enough. When, soon after, I was about to leave Moscow Count Schulenburg gave me a farewell dinner. At the beginning he rose to his feet and said, 'Our young friend Hayter tells me he has never eaten his fill of oysters. I have sent for a barrel of them from the Baltic, and we will now test his capacity.' I ate three and a half dozen.

Among the less important papers found when the archives of the German Foreign Office were seized by the Allies after the war was the following letter from the German Embassy in Moscow to the Ministry of Foreign Affairs in Berlin:

January 11th, 1937

Subject: Third Secretary Hayter's transfer to London

William G. Hayter, who has been Third Secretary at the British Embassy here for nearly two years, has been recalled to the Foreign Office. He will work there in the League of Nations Department under Mr. Strang, formerly Counsellor in Moscow.

Before his appointment to Moscow Mr. Hayter was attached to the British Legation in Vienna. There he was very intimate with members of the Austrian aristocracy. During his stay in Austria he learned excellent German, which he speaks fluently with a slight Viennese accent.

Mr. Hayter is in the early thirties and unmarried. Besides German he speaks good French; his knowledge of Russian is not very extensive.

His gay and likeable personality made him a favourite of great popularity in the Moscow Diplomatic Corps. Without adopting the German attitude towards the Soviet Union and Communism, his standpoint towards the state of affairs here was critical.

2*

Mr. Hayter maintained close and friendly connections with the younger members of the German Embassy. Thus opportunities frequently arose to talk on political matters with him. In such conversations he showed himself candid and communicative. Even though on occasion his opinions did not coincide with the views put forward by us, Mr. Hayter still displayed understanding for the German standpoint. During my last trip to the Caucasus, on which Mr. Hayter accompanied me, I got to know him well and to esteem him as an able young diplomat.

Before he left Mr. Hayter expressed the hope that his friendly relations with the German Embassy in Moscow might be maintained with the staff of the German Embassy in London. I trust that our London Embassy will do its utmost to encourage Mr. Hayter in this endeavour.

(Sgd.) Schulenburg.

To: The Foreign Ministry
　　Berlin.

I read this voice from the tomb in 1946 with mixed feelings. It was far too flattering, of course. But no diplomat likes to see himself described as 'communicative', and it was perhaps as well for me that Ribbentrop never followed up Count Schulenburg's recommendation to cultivate me. Count Schulenburg was certainly justified in describing my attitude to the state of affairs in Moscow as critical. There was plenty to be critical about, at that time. The assassination of Kirov in December 1934, some months after my arrival, had been the signal for the first of Stalin's great purges. The trial of Kamenev and Zinoviev took place in my time in Moscow, and I recollect drafting for Lord Chilston what was no doubt a very callow despatch about it, using the traditional cliché about revolution devouring its children. But my unformed views about that catastrophic period of history are of little interest at this distance. My role was a very minor one, and my detachment seems to have worn thin fairly early. In the last letter I wrote Sligger shortly before his death, soon after my arrival in Moscow, I described the Soviet Union as 'a cruel and heartless tyranny', which though accurate enough as applied to Stalinism does not suggest an altogether detached view. During one of my leaves I visited Oxford and stayed with the Haldanes. H. W. B. Joseph, my former philosophy tutor, dined with them one night. I was airing my famous open mind on Russia to him when he asked me 'Is there a rule of law there?' On reflexion I saw that this was the right question and that the unquestionably correct negative answer told one nearly all one needed to know of Stalin's Russia.

My chief regret about my first period in the Soviet Union is my failure to learn Russian properly. I was transferred to Moscow at short notice, with no time off to learn the language, and I have reluctantly concluded that Russian is not a language one can acquire in one's spare time. I took intermittent lessons from a series of teachers in Moscow, but there was little scope for prac- tising it and I never became fluent; I was to regret this failure when, some twenty years later, I was again sent to Moscow with no time off for language instruction.

Moscow was not a popular post in the thirties, and it was accepted that after two years one had a right to a transfer. Lord Chilston asked me if I wished to exercise this right, and I said I should much prefer to stay on; I was finding life both interesting and enjoyable. However after another six months I was told I was to be transferred to the League of Nations Section of the Foreign Office, and I started there early in 1937. This seemed to me an attractive prospect; I had found my brief visit to Geneva in 1931 full of interest, and membership of the League of Nations Section meant contact with senior members of the Service and frequent journeys to Geneva in the company of the Foreign Secretary, all good for promotion. Alethea, then working for *Country Life*, and I took a flat in Westminster together and I used to walk daily to the Foreign Office across a corner of St. James's Park, when I was not away at Geneva.

It is interesting to reflect on the differing ways in which the League of Nations and its successor, the United Nations, impinged or impinge on the Foreign Office. On the one hand the Foreign Secretary, often with other senior members of the Government, regularly attended League of Nations meetings, whereas his appearance at the United Nations is an event. On the other hand, while now the Foreign Office maintains several large departments to deal with United Nations affairs, and a powerful permanent delegation in New York, in League of Nations days all this work was done by the three officials of the League of Nations Section, a sub-section of the Western Department, who dealt with all the papers at the London end and who went in a body to Geneva for sessions of the League Council and Assembly. When this happened a junior in the Western Department was supposed to act as rear link; in my time this was Charles Johnston, who confined his activities to marking all the papers that came to him 'Mr. Hayter on return'.

The same bureaucratic inflation has of course infected the international organizations themselves. During my time at Geneva the Palais des Nations was inaugurated to house the League Secretariat and to provide meeting rooms for the Council and Assembly. It was then regarded as an enormous white elephant. Today it houses, with difficulty, a minor off-shoot of the United Nations.

Though so grandly housed, by the standards of the 1930's, the League had declined catastrophically in prestige and self-confidence since my time there in 1931. Germany, Italy and Japan had left, and the adherence of the Soviet Union hardly compensated for their absence in the estimation of those days. The Council spent most of its time listening helplessly to appeals for assistance from China and Republican Spain. They could do nothing for either. If they could have chosen they might have preferred China, because Wellington Koo, who represented it, was an intelligent charmer, not epithets one would have applied to the Republican Spanish representative Alvarez del Vayo. But in fact they were equally impotent in both cases. The League's total impotence had just been blindingly revealed over Abyssinia. This allowed me to witness an interesting episode. The question of raising sanctions against Italy was under discussion in the Council soon after I joined the League of Nations Section, and the Emperor Haile Selassie, then in exile, demanded to be heard in person. Before the hearing the Council discussed, in private session, how he should be treated. Was he a Head of State? Or was he merely the representative of the former Abyssinian Government? If the former we should rise to our feet on his entry, if the latter not. It was decided that he was clearly no more than the representative of the dispossessed Government, so we should not rise. The Council then went into public session, and the Emperor was admitted. He paused at the door, a small, impressive, cloaked figure, and looked at us. We all shambled to our feet.

This period of the League's decadence was not an agreeable one for those who had to take part in it. Writing to my mother in January 1935 I said, 'We're having a very bad Geneva, everything seems to be going wrong and the deepest pessimism prevails. We no longer hope to do any good and concentrate on preventing really bad things. All the little countries like Turkey and Roumania spend their time blackmailing the French and ourselves by threatening that if we don't give in to their discreditable ramps they will go over to the Rome–Berlin axis.'

There were some interludes in this depressing attendance on the League's decline. One was the coronation of King George VI, at which I had a very minor place in attendance on the Secretary-General of the League of Nations, Joseph Avenol. The heartfelt prayer of all of us allocated to attendance of this kind was 'Long may he reign'. All busy men working in various government departments, we were constantly summoned to meetings at St. James's Palace by courtiers who would themselves fail to turn up or who, if they did condescend to appear, seemed to be half-witted. The exception was the Duke of Norfolk, then organizing his first major ceremony, who struck us all as brisk, competent and professional. After all the preliminary muddle the ceremony itself went astonishingly well, so far as I could see it from my remote seat in the Abbey; the sound of the silver trumpets at the critical moment was among the most moving I have ever heard.

Another interlude, of a quite different kind, occurred in the spring of 1938 when I was sent for a month's spell in Republican Spain to relieve a secretary, badly in need of leave, at the British Embassy, which had settled down in a village called Caldetas on the coast east of Barcelona. The Republic was by then reduced to a small area round Barcelona, and its end was obviously at hand. Like most people in the Foreign Office, I took this less tragically than the British public as a whole, particularly its left wing. Young intellectuals, who had regarded the destruction of Abyssinia with frigid indifference and who thought the German reoccupation of the Rhineland on the whole a good thing, suddenly felt that the fate of the whole free world was at stake in the Spanish Civil War and hurried bravely off to take part in it. In the Foreign Office we thought the real battle was elsewhere. But I was quite glad to have a look at close hand at this conflict which so impassioned my contemporaries.

When I got to Caldetas, however, there was not much sign of war. Indeed the only visible battle was that between the British Embassy and the Royal Navy. The Navy accused the Embassy of panicking, while the Embassy thought the guard-ships off shore were slack about passing on our cipher messages and watched with some embarrassment the unsuccessful attempts of the sailors to put a boat ashore on the sandy beach at Caldetas. Nevertheless it was reassuring to see the great grey silhouette of *Hood* or *Repulse* lying off our rather nervous village. It was peaceful enough by day, but by night unexplained shots would be heard, and sometimes our windows would rattle as Franco's little aeroplanes from the Balearic Islands dropped bombs on Barcelona. These bombs did not seem to disturb the nightingales, which sang on unperturbed in the little copse by the villa in which I was quartered; indeed Spanish nightingales appeared to me to be rather brazen creatures, singing so loud that I could hardly sleep and not even stopping by day; every bush in the drive up to the Minister's villa seemed to contain one, perched on a conspicuous twig, its throat feathers vibrating as it poured out its vigorous song.

Inside, the Minister's villa was full of duchesses. They had taken refuge there, and stayed till an exchange against left-wing captives could be arranged for them through the British mission to Franco. The Minister used to lecture them about Franco's iniquities; they did not dare to contradict him, for fear of being turned out. These exchanges seemed to be the Embassy's main function. Every so often one would be arranged, and we would go into Barcelona and see them off, the duchesses being joined by parties of nuns, one of whom would generally turn out to be a priest in disguise. When the party was finally sorted out it would go off to a British warship, passing under the stern of one of the prison-ships moored in the harbour, where dirty, unshaven sentries patrolled the barbed-wire decks. Apart from these exchanges there was not much for the Embassy to do. We used to go into Barcelona occasionally for rather futile interviews with Alvares del Vayo and his disintegrating Ministry, and once there was a dismal little reception to celebrate the anniversary of the Republic, on that day when, in my first year in the Foreign Office, I had heard over the telephone from Madrid the shouting crowds pro-claiming the downfall of the Monarchy. There was not, I told my mother in a letter from Caldetas, a pane of glass left in the centre of Barcelona; 'some buildings have disappeared entirely, and there are great holes in the roadway. The town looks hot, dusty and bedraggled, but most of the shops are open and people seem to go about in an ordinary way: there are very long bread queues, longer than any I saw in Moscow. We don't see or hear much of the war here,' I went on, 'though troops and guns pass fairly often through the village. Sometimes we hear distant thumps and thuds which are supposed to be from the fighting round Lerida. Yesterday there was a small air-raid at Motaró, a town about ten miles from here on the road to Barcelona: about 8.30 in the morning I was reading in bed when I heard aeroplanes very loud, then there were some loud thuds, the windows rattled and the electric light went out. It was a lovely sunny morning and the birds were singing. We spent this morning prospecting the mountains inland for an alternative route to Barcelona avoiding the coastal towns: not only are they liable to be bombed but the roads through them are very narrow and might be jammed if there was a panic exodus from Barcelona: we want to be able to bring out the 300 British subjects still in Barcelona to Caldetas if the worst comes to the worst. We didn't find a very satisfactory route but we had a lovely drive through mountain-country, and through valleys full of wild cherry and almond-blossom; it was hard to believe there was a war on.' In another letter to my mother I reported that the Admiral had promised us a guard-ship at Caldetas every other day, 'so we must hope the trouble won't start on the other day'. However my month in Spain ended

without any trouble at all, and I returned to London just in time
to set off to Geneva with the Foreign Secretary at the beginning of
May.

The Foreign Secretary when I began my spell at the Foreign
Office was Anthony Eden, who was replaced after a year by Lord
Halifax, much to the general disgust of most Foreign Office
officials. We had all deplored what we considered the weakness of
the Conservative Government's policy over Abyssinia and in relation to the European dictatorships in general; we regarded Eden's
tenure of the Foreign Office as a sign that this process might be
reversed, and his removal as a sign that it would not be. Even at
my lowly level I was aware of the kind of feeling among the
senior officials which is so vividly portrayed in Oliver Harvey's
diaries. But it made little actual difference to my own work
except that it was now Lord Halifax and not Mr. Eden who led
our little parties to Geneva at recurrent intervals.

On one such occasion Lord Halifax, contemplating me gloomily
on the platform at Victoria, suddenly startled me by saying, 'Are
you a relation of Cecil Griffin?' Griffin had been his private secretary when he was Viceroy of India, and Lord Halifax apparently
thought that I resembled him. I said I was no relation, and did not
add that I was trying to become his brother-in-law. He was in fact a
half-brother of Iris Hoare, with whom I had skied at Wengen so
many years before and of whom I had begun to see quite a lot
recently. On leaves from Moscow we had again skied together at
Kitzbühel and Zürs, and I had stayed with her father and step-
mother at Hocker Edge, their house in Kent. Charles Grey, her
father (he had had to change his name when his second wife became tenant for life of a Grey property), was one of the few men
to take an active part in the Boer War, the First World War and
the Second World War. In the intervals between wars he became
a famous gardener, winning Gold Cups at the Chelsea Flower
Show from his Kent garden, writing a three-volume work on hardy
bulbs, and founding, after the Second World War, the Northern
Horticultural Society's gardens at Harlow Car. He was also, at
different times, an unsuccessful candidate for Parliament in the
Labour and in the Conservative interest. During his Labour
phase Iris had been sent to Bedales, and she subsequently got an

economics degree at Cambridge. We became engaged in the early summer of 1938, soon after my return from Spain; this was undoubtedly the wisest decision I ever took.

Shortly after Iris had accepted me I was told by Derick Hoyer-Millar, the Private Secretary who then dealt with diplomatic appointments, that I was to be appointed to the Embassy in China. I told him I had just got engaged. 'Not to a foreigner, I hope?' he asked; I was able to reassure him by telling him Iris was a niece of Rex Hoare, then Minister in Bucharest. It was settled that I should go to the League Assembly in September, we would be married when I got back and would leave for China immediately thereafter.

This League Assembly turned out to be very different from the last one that I had attended. The 1937 Assembly had coincided with the opening of the Palais des Nations, and the Aga Khan, President of the Assembly that year, had given an enormous ball in the new building, with lavish supplies of champagne which were wheeled round on the trolleys more normally used for transporting League documents. The 1938 Assembly met under the shadow of the Munich crisis. De Valera, the President that year, gave a very austere reception in a hotel; there was no champagne and all the carpets were left down to ensure that there would be no dancing. The Foreign Secretary was not at Geneva nor was any member of the Cabinet. Litvinov, then Soviet Foreign Minister and head of the Soviet delegation, hung about in Geneva, obviously making himself available for a British approach that never came. Night after night we would listen to Hitler's horrible voice ranting over the radio. After one such speech I went out on to a balcony of the hotel to breathe some decent air. Geneva was having a practice black-out and the town was under a heavy black pall, but away to the north the sky was glowing inexplicably, brilliantly red. We heard next day that it was an abnormal aurora borealis, but at the time it seemed a ghastly portent. Soon after Iris rang up from London. Did I, she asked, see any hope of avoiding war? I said I didn't. I couldn't see how an issue at once peaceful and honourable was possible. When, a few days later, an issue came that was peaceful and not honourable I felt a kind of shamefaced relief because at least it meant that

our wedding arrangements could go ahead. We were married in
Kent, on a beautiful October day, and after a few days by the sea
at Birchington and farewell visits to our two families set off for
China.

FOUR

A Married Man

An attentive reader, if any there be, may have observed a certain vagueness about the dates in this narrative hitherto. This is because, up to this point, I have had to rely on my not very reliable memory, with occasional quotations from my letters to my mother, all of which she religiously kept. From now on, everything changes. My mother kept a diary all her life, and practically the only advice she ever gave to Iris, when we were engaged, was that she too should keep a diary. This Iris has faithfully done, and so from this point I can practically always (for we have very seldom been apart for long) verify what I was doing, where I was, whom I met at any point of time. Iris's diary was always left lying about and so records primarily events, not opinions, but it provides an invaluable framework.

Before the Second World War when people in our walk of life got married *The Times* and other newspapers used to send to the prospective bride a large questionnaire covering such matters as bridesmaids, guests at the wedding, wedding presents and so on. The results were published in full in the newspapers. One of the questions asked was about the location of the honeymoon. Birchington, we thought, sounded rather unglamorous, so under this heading we wrote India, where we were in fact intending to spend ten days staying with Cecil Griffin, then working in the Political Department in New Delhi. We went that far by air, in those days still something of an adventure and much more interesting than it is now, because the aeroplanes flew lower and one saw so much more of the country. The Dutch plane which took us involved spending nights on the ground at Rotterdam, Naples, Alexandria, and Basra. Almost all the way we could get clear views of the land and sea below, instead of the monotonous cloudscapes that are now the staple of air travel. I remember, as we left Basra, looking down on the dwellings of the Marsh Arabs in the delta of the Shatt-el-Arab. We were living in an uncertain world then and our own personal future was obscure; but I thought to myself that whatever happened to us we could always remember someone worse off than ourselves, the Marsh Arabs of Southern Iraq. Later, we flew so low that we could see the sharks lying off the rocks in the clear waters of the Indian Ocean.

New Delhi, when we arrived there on a day of brilliant, cool, winter sunshine, seemed to bask in the secure glow of an un-shakeable Raj. We watched Cecil play polo in the shadow of Humayun's tomb, and admired the splendours of the Viceroy's House, which seemed, and still seems, to me the only really grand palace built in this century, the culmination of a lay-out nobler than Versailles, the supreme expression of triumphant imperialism just before its close and entirely worthy to become, as it now has, the residence of the Head of State of a major power. Delhi, and Agra which we also briefly visited, were not less noticeable for the architectural triumphs of another imperialism, that of the Moghuls. Aldous Huxley and Robert Byron were then teaching us to despise Moghul architecture; Byron proclaimed that the only decent Muslim architecture was to be found in the more inaccessible regions of Oxiana, while Huxley described the Taj Mahal (which Iris and I visited by the light of a full moon, in the traditional honeymoon manner) as an expensive disappointment and its minarets 'among the ugliest structures ever erected by human hands'. I did my best to convince myself that I had these fashionable feelings, but could not manage not to be impressed. Later acquaintance with other Muslim architecture elsewhere, in Iran, Soviet Central Asia and the Maghreb, reinforced my view that the Moghul buildings at Delhi and Agra are the handsomest, as they undoubtedly are the largest and the most lavish, put up by Mahomedan architects anywhere, with the possible exception of Sinan's mosques in Istanbul.

After Delhi and Agra we took a train to Bombay and boarded the P. & O. *Corfu* for Shanghai. This was an agreeable voyage. There were different delicious curries for dinner every night, and at each port at which we touched different delicious exotic fruits would be brought on board. These ports, Colombo, Penang, Singapore, Hong Kong, were then all parts of the British colonial empire. As such they were undeniably impressive. One would steam for days past empty green coasts, the only sign of human life being the occasional fishing boat or impoverished fishing villages, wooden huts on stilts. Then the ship would round a cape and there would suddenly appear a modern town, with a domed law-court, a spired cathedral, a pillared legislature, a busy port, streets, buses, policemen, crowded shops and solid houses, all rather graceless perhaps but busy and real and an amazing contrast with the lifeless land around them, something created out of nothing by purposeful activity. The British Empire brought many evils in its train and its disappearance seems to me a welcome phenomenon, but I find it impossible to regret that it should ever have been; without it those endless green coasts would still lie as lifeless as ever.

Our approach to Hong Kong was beset by an unusual problem. Some Royal personage, the Queen of Norway if I remember rightly, had died, and court mourning was proclaimed. I knew what this meant for me as a bachelor, a black tie every day and no parties, but what did it imply for Iris? Did she, for instance, have to wear black stockings? The problem was urgent because Iris was anxious to land correctly dressed at her first diplomatic post. Could one, if they were necessary (and who could say if they were or not?) buy black stockings in Hong Kong? Such are, or were in those days, the minor problems of diplomatic life. I forget how we solved this one, but I know it meant that poor Iris could not dazzle Shanghai with her new trousseau for several weeks.

We got to Shanghai at the end of November, and after a month in the gloomy luxury of the Cathay Hotel installed ourselves in a little house in the French Concession. The house was all half-timbering and lattice windows, like a villa in Putney or North Oxford in its main structure; but attached to it by one corner was another building which contained our enormous staff, the No. 1 boy and No. 2 boy, the cook and the learner cook, the amah, the coolie, the gardener, the chauffeur, most of them with large families (the No. 1 boy had two wives). Quei, the No. 1 boy, was a remarkable character. He had been the head

servant in the flagship of the flotilla of British gun-boats which
patrolled the Yangtse. He had found this position an excellent one
for organizing opium-smuggling up and down the river. When
this was detected he was dismissed, whereupon he withdrew all
Chinese labour from the gun-boats, thus effectively immobilizing
them. 'Face' clearly precluded his re-employment in the flagship,
but was saved by the provision of a suitable situation for him in
the Embassy, which being immobile provided less scope for
opium-smuggling. We were delighted to inherit him from a
member of the Embassy who was going on leave. He was an
elderly gentleman of immense charm and dignity, who organized
our large household with smooth efficiency. We thus started our
married life with a degree of luxury, on the domestic front, that
we were never to attain again except, passingly, in the Embassy
in Moscow.

The situation in China was then a peculiar one. The Japanese
pressure on China, beginning with the Mukden incident which
had troubled the end of my first visit to the League of Nations in
1931, had since 1937 become the full-scale war that the League
had been able to do so little about during my second Geneva
period. By the time we reached Shanghai the Japanese had occupied all the main cities and treaty-ports in China, with the exception of one or two international enclaves, and the Chinese
Government had been driven into the interior and had established
itself at Chungking, the most remote of all the treaty-ports, on
the upper Yangtse above the gorges and beyond a range of
mountains which the Japanese had not been able to penetrate. But
between the main cities, even in the coastal areas, most of the
territory was controlled by various Chinese guerrilla forces, and
though the Japanese could easily defeat any Chinese army they
met in the field and could hold the main centres they were never
able to control the country as a whole. They had set up a puppet
Government in Nanking, under one of the principal leaders of
the Kuomintang, Wang Ching-wei, but this Government was
recognized by no one but themselves and had few adherents and
no prestige. The main leaders of the Kuomintang, the party which
had more or less governed China since 1927, were in Chungking
with Chiang Kai-shek, maintaining an uneasy relationship with

the Chinese communists who by then were still further up country; their liaison officer in Chungking was a clever young man called Chou En-lai.

The Kuomintang was a peculiar organization. I was much struck, when I first came to know about it, by the closeness with which its structure and organization was modelled on that of the Soviet Communist party, familiar to me from my Moscow days. But its ideology was very different. It was a strongly nationalist body, radical and republican in its origins, with overtones of Wesleyan-Methodist puritanism, but gradually, with the extension of its power, becoming more and more capitalist and increasingly corrupt. It had for years been conducting a campaign on a number of fronts, against local war-lords, against the imperialist powers which had a stranglehold on China's economy, particularly Japan, and against the Chinese Communist Party with which it had at first been in alliance but which had since become its most deadly internal enemy. It was dominated by what was often known as the Soong Dynasty. This was the family of Madame Chiang Kai-shek, always referred to by foreigners as Madame *tout court*. One of her sisters was the widow of Sun Yet-sen, the founding father of the Chinese Republic. Another was married to H. H. Kung, a lineal descendant of Confucius, who had held various financial positions and was, when we arrived in China, Prime Minister (Chiang Kai-shek was President and Generalissimo). A brother, T. V. Soong, was Finance Minister; he was on bad terms with his brother-in-law the Prime Minister and was usually in the United States.

The role of the British Embassy in this situation was not easy. It was nominally accredited to the Kuomintang government in Chungking. But its main task was the protection of the immense British commercial interests in China, and these were mainly situated in the treaty-ports, all with the exception of Chungking in Japanese hands. It is hard to visualize, in these days of diminished British power, how great the British stake in China then was, far greater and more widespread than that of any other Power except, perhaps, Japan. Shanghai was the financial, commercial and industrial centre of China, and its core was the International Settlement, composed of an amalgamation of the former British and American Concessions. The Bund, its water-front and main street, was dominated, indeed monopolized, by British concerns, from the British Consulate-General at one end to the Shanghai Club (containing what was reputed to be the longest bar in the world) at the other. On a smaller scale the same situation was repeated in every treaty-port; in the lesser ones the British Consulate was the pre-eminent building of the whole town. The coastal shipping trade and even the river shipping on the Yangtse were largely in British hands. Great British firms like British-American Tobacco and Asiatic Petroleum maintained distributing agencies throughout the country. The British colony in Shanghai was one of the largest in the world. This rich but vulnerable investment was insecurely protected by a substantial but still inadequate fleet based on the Crown Colony of Hong Kong (with a summer station at the leased island of Weihaiwei in the north), and by small garrisons ashore in Shanghai and the British Concession at Tientsin. The Japanese were everywhere leaning on this British domain, encircling the concessions and settlements, interfering with British trade and shipping, harassing British subjects. The Chinese Government, far away in Chungking, could do nothing about this situation but, not unnaturally, objected to an Embassy accredited to it having any dealings with the Japanese with whom it was at war.

The Embassy, equally naturally, could not altogether accept this objection, but organized itself in a rather special way to deal with it. Its main offices were in the International Settlement in Shanghai. It had withdrawn entirely from Nanking, then the official capital, in order to avoid any contact with Wang Ching-wei's puppet régime there. A rump remained in Peking, the old capital and the seat of the Legation Quarter, mainly consisting of cadet members of the China Consular Service learning the language. A small outpost, known as the Diplomatic Mission, was in Chungking, and the Ambassador divided his time between Chungking and Shanghai.

The Ambassador at this time, Sir Archibald Clark Kerr (afterwards Lord Inverchapel) was a remarkable man and rather an odd character. He had many defects. He was something of a bully and a tease; his first invitation to us on our arrival was not to his house but to a Chinese restaurant where we were forced, under his critical eye, to manipulate chopsticks for the first time, and the dangling sleeves of Iris's elegant blouse kept dipping into the delicious dishes. He had various affectations; for instance he would only write with a quill pen, and keeping him supplied with goose-quills in war-time Chungking imposed a tiresome and unnecessary burden on his staff. He was very vain of his appearance and took endless pains, with the help of masseurs, to keep his figure trim. He was not good on paper, and almost all his drafting was done by his staff. But with all these flaws he remained a powerful Ambassador. He impressed his personality, so that you could not help competing for his favours. Most foreigners in China in those days thought the avenue to influence was by pleasing Madame; but Clark Kerr somehow created the impression that he didn't take her seriously, so she found herself trying to please him. He affected left-wing views, and said openly that Chou En-lai was worth all the Kuomintang rolled together (he was quite right, of course). He was later Ambassador in Moscow, and in my time there Mikoyan and the other Soviet leaders used to say he was the best British Ambassador they had known (their opinion of his predecessor, Stafford Cripps, was I fear not high). His last post was as Ambassador in Washington. Here he was less of a success. I once asked Joe Alsop how he was doing. 'Not well,' said Joe. 'There are two things wrong. He makes jokes, and they don't always come off. And he doesn't suffer fools gladly; there are many important fools in Washington.' But in China and Moscow he was very effective.

The personnel of the Embassy in China was then drawn from two quite different sources. The Ambassador and most of his diplomatic staff were members of the Diplomatic Service; they were generalists who came to China for a short spell, probably did not know the language and expected to spend most of their careers elsewhere. Then there were the specialists, members of the China Consular Service, who occupied the posts of Chinese Counsellor, Chinese Secretary and Private Secretary to the Ambassador. Other members of this Service staffed the Consulates. They had all been given two years' language training in Peking and were expected to pass most if not all of their careers in China.

They were there to provide the local knowledge and the language; the generalists were to provide a wider perspective. This was not a very just or efficient system, and it led to friction if the personalities were wrong, but it was not entirely without its justification. China specialists, including China Consuls, tended to go to one extreme or the other; either they were passionately Sinophile or they loathed everything Chinese. The generalists did perhaps, though ignorant, retain slightly more detachment and a better sense of the relation of China's problems to those of the rest of the world.

From both these sets of problems the life we found ourselves leading in Shanghai seemed very remote. It was intensely social, in rather a provincial way. The world of the International Settlement and the French Concession in Shanghai was not to me an attractive one. It was a get-rich-quick world. Social conscience was not at a premium, and the town was singularly graceless. There were few public amenities, the main exception being the subsidized Shanghai Municipal Orchestra, which though not perhaps a close rival of the Vienna Philharmonic was then the only professional orchestra in Asia performing the classical repertoire. The Municipality made few other concessions to the graces. The only public open space, Jessfield Park, was the venue of the notorious 'Dogs and Chinese not admitted' notice. It was not put quite as crudely as that, but a long list of park regulations posted at the gate said in one paragraph 'Dogs not admitted' and in another 'This park is reserved for the use of the European population'. This was not untypical of the European attitude; white men kicking rickshaw coolies were a common spectacle. When not engaged in this satisfying pastime the Europeans spent what little time they could spare from amassing large fortunes in frenzied social activities. We found ourselves inevitably involved in these. There were endless dinner-parties. Conversation after dinner was inconceivable in so unintellectual a world, so the moment dinner was over bridge began, or the party moved off to a film or a nightclub, or both in succession. A few Chinese, of the play-boy type, took part in all this, but mostly it was China merchants, mainly British, with a sprinkling of diplomats and foreign correspondents. After a bit we began to sort out a few of the younger ones who were more civilized, and of course there were shining exceptions like the Keswick brothers, and correspondents like Christopher Chancellor and Ian Morrison. But I still treasure the memory of a dinner given at the Embassy for Stafford Cripps who arrived unexpectedly in one of his family's ships. The Chargé d'Affaires assembled the heads of most of the British firms to meet him. Over the port, when conversation became general, Sir Stafford said in his mild, precise voice, 'Of course you are all here to exploit the Chinese.' The ensuing explosion was a pleasure to watch.

All this intense social and commercial activity went on within a strictly limited area. The Japanese had surrounded the international sectors with a closely-guarded barbed-wire perimeter. It was possible to pass through this at one or two points, particularly to go to Hungjao where a few foreigners still lived in splendid villas and where the only remaining golf-course (there had been four) functioned on sufferance. Further round was the suburb of Chapei, the scene of fierce fighting in 1937 and now utterly desolate; it was strange to look across its flattened, burnt-out houses and factories at the luxurious Shanghai skyscrapers where, one knew, at that very moment a rich and apparently carefree life was carrying on. Shanghai was then like an island; it was possible to take a few country walks at Hungjao, through flat fields smelling of human excrement, but the beautiful near-by towns, Hangchow and Soochow, were inaccessible and travel in the rest of China virtually impossible. The Japanese could not admit that they were unable to control the countryside, mostly in guerrilla hands, and so refused travel permits, arresting those like the British Military Attaché who tried to travel without a permit. As a result, though we were able to pay a short visit to Peking, we left China without having seen the Great Wall, the Ming Tombs or the Yangtse gorges, a great blow to a dedicated sightseer like me.

Still, it was something to have seen Peking. There still remained there then some of those European travellers who, on journeys round the world, had meant to spend a few days in Peking and who had been there ever since. One could quite see why. Not only is it among the most beautiful, and the best planned, cities in the world, in the class of Leningrad or Isfahan, but it also then had still a most agreeable life, delicious restaurants, marvellous curio shops, an ample supply of the best domestic servants in the world, heavenly country near by and a decent climate. This was all marred during our visit by the Japanese occupiers, fierce ugly little men with gauze masks over their mouths and noses, but enough remained for us to be able to understand Peking's potent attraction.

This was the only time we got away from Shanghai during our first year in China. For the rest, we stayed on our artificial island and worked away in our different ways. Iris, always strong on good works, managed even in Shanghai to combine them with our intense social life. One particular cause took a lot of her time. Shanghai was then one of the few places in the world that German Jews could enter without a visa, and every liner from Europe would bring hundreds of them, allowed by the Nazis to book passages and bring a few personal possessions but nothing else, so that they stepped off the ships beautifully dressed but penniless. The small existing Jewish community in Shanghai did what it could but other help was needed, and Iris was much involved in this. The refugees from Germany, mostly able professional people, soon established themselves catering in various ways to Shanghai's rich foreigners, unfortunately in strong and often successful competition with Shanghai's other refugee community, the White Russians, who had been gradually building up little trades, as dressmakers and restaurant-keepers for instance, since the exodus from Siberia enforced by the Russian Revolution, and who now found themselves outbid by the newly arrived and more energetic German Jews.

My own work was intense in different ways. Iris's diary records, for practically every Sunday morning, 'Went to church, W. to office'. I was working a six-and-a-half day week, in fact. The crisis that was building up to the outbreak of war in Europe was having its repercussions in the Far East. British strength was dangerously over-extended, and was clearly inadequate to protect the rich British holdings in China. The Japanese could see this, and were closing in for the kill. There were other problems, the most acute being the Burma Road, the only land communication between the territory held by the Chungking government and the outside world, which the Japanese were pressing us to close and the Chinese to develop. In dealing with all these problems the British Embassies in Japan and China were getting at cross-purposes. The Ambassador in Tokyo, Sir Robert Craigie, was pressing the British Government to make the best possible bargain with the Japanese. Clark Kerr saw no future in this and thought that on the contrary we should help the Chinese to defeat the Japanese and drive them out of China. In an attempt to resolve these differences a kind of summit meeting of Ambassadors was arranged. Clark Kerr could not go to Japan without destroying his position in China, but Craigie could come to Japanese-held Shanghai without compromising himself, and he and Lady Craigie arrived there at the beginning of April. The visit was not a success. Craigie was stiff, formal and rather pompous; Clark Kerr was elaborately informal, and to their political differences personal incompatibilities were now added. Lady Clark Kerr was away, and as everyone senior to me on the Embassy staff was a bachelor, Iris found herself looking after Lady Craigie. This led to an invitation to us to visit them in Tokyo, which we accepted in spite of Clark Kerr's disapproval of his staff associating with someone he now regarded as the enemy.

When we arrived in Japan at the end of August we went almost straight up to Chuzenji, the mountain resort where most of the Tokyo Embassies had summer houses, passing on the way through Nikko which struck us as very vulgar and tawdry by comparison with the noble grandeur of Peking. Chuzenji was deliciously cool after the sweltering heat of Shanghai and Tokyo. The Craigies had remained in Tokyo; every morning their Japanese chef would submit to us enormous menus written out in French (which he did not know) for lunch and dinner; we would cross off most of the dishes but always leave on the delicious fresh-caught trout from the lake. Charles Johnston, then Third Secretary in Tokyo, joined us and took us sailing on the lake or for cruises in the Embassy launch, known as the Saloon of Death owing to its top-heavy glass superstructure. This agreeable idyll was interrupted by increasingly serious news from Europe and by two telegrams from Clark Kerr, the first telling me he intended to take me with him to Chungking at the end of September, and the second

ordering me to return to Shanghai immediately. We cancelled a
projected visit to Kyoto and booked a passage on the next ship
back from Kobe (there was then no air service between Japan
and China).

We left Kobe in the C.P.R. liner *Empress of Asia* on the afternoon of September 1st. As we set sail the big German liner
Scharnhorst, which had left Kobe the day before for Singapore and
Europe, returned to take refuge in the Japanese waters. Next day
we heard of the ultimatum to Germany, and that evening I and one
or two other British passengers were summoned by the captain,
who informed us that there were more Germans than British
subjects on board this British-registered ship and that he was not
quite certain what the position would be if war were declared.
The C.P.R. liners then had British officers but Asian crews, and it
seemed that we and the officers were outnumbered by the German
passengers, who might try to take over the ship. It was not quite
clear what the captain wanted us to do about this, but we looked
appropriately solemn and resolute. Next morning, as we crossed
the China Sea, we saw two Japanese destroyers approaching very
rapidly on our port quarter. It was not at all certain then that the
Japanese would not declare war on Great Britain as soon as Germany did, and we watched the destroyers' approach with some
trepidation. However they nipped across our bow and continued
northwards, and next day we docked in Shanghai without incident; the German passengers were mostly harmless missionaries
returning to their posts after a summer holiday in the Japanese
mountains.

A day or two later I went to see the Ambassador and told him
I thought I ought to resign and join the army, or something.
After all, I said, I was only 33, and I'd got Certificate A at Winchester which was supposed to be precisely for this kind of situation. The Ambassador pooh-poohed this quite kindly; in any
case, he said, he'd had strict instructions from the Foreign Office
that no members of the Diplomatic Service were to be allowed to
resign and join the forces. Besides, I was urgently needed in
Chungking. I must admit I heard all this with great relief. I was
convinced I should make a very incompetent soldier, and I
seemed to be turning into a fairly efficient diplomat. Moreover,

Iris was expecting a baby in April and this wouldn't be a good moment for us to be separated.

However a brief separation was now inevitable. When I left with the Ambassador for Chungking Iris came with us as far as Hong Kong, where she was to stay in the marble splendours of Admiralty House with Sir Percy and Lady Noble while I flew off with Clark Kerr and the rest of his entourage to Chungking, over the top of the Sino-Japanese war raging, rather mildly, below us in Kwantung. We arrived in Chungking early in the morning of October 7th, landing on a sand-bank in the Yangtse. The wheel by then had hardly reached Chungking, and we were carried up the steep bank from the airport in sedan-chairs and had to take to them again, after a short car-ride, to reach the British Consulate-General, which was in a narrow lane, interspersed with steps, that even a rickshaw could not penetrate.

The old city of Chungking was built on a rocky promontory between the Yangtse and one of its tributaries, the Chialing. Its narrow paved lanes and flights of steps ran steeply up and down between ramshackle wooden houses. The British Consulate-General, near the top of the rock, consisted of two substantial houses, one for the Consul-General and one for the Vice-Consul, on opposite sides of one of these narrow lanes, each with a big garden and a fine southward view to the Yangtse and the tree-fringed hills on the south bank. An air-raid shelter, connected to the two houses, had been blasted out of the solid rock under the dividing lane. In this little compound the Ambassador and his party lived and worked, overcrowding the consular occupants. A tenuous connexion with the outside world was maintained through the wireless of a British gunboat moored on the Yangtse far below, and occasional diplomatic bags reached us via the precarious airline to Hong Kong or, for heavy stuff, the Burma Road or a lorry-service from the rail-head of the Indo-China railway that led up from Haiphong into South-east China.

The Ambassador's intention was to stay a few weeks in Chung-king and then return to Shanghai, leaving me in charge of the Diplomatic Mission. But at first he did not seem to have much for me to do, so I asked if I could take a trip down the Yangtse on one of the British steamers still running on the upper river. Clark

Kerr forbade this, saying I must stay in Chungking and get to know the Chinese, and soon afterwards took me off to dinner with the Chiang Kai-sheks. This was an interesting evening. Clark Kerr was at his game of teasing Madame. In those days it was a great mark of favour in Chungking to receive a present of fudge, allegedly made by Madame's own fair hand. Clark Kerr told her he was sure this was all nonsense and that the fudge was in fact made by some of her countless minions. To prove him wrong Madame ordered some of the said countless minions to bring in a chafing dish and the materials for fudge-making. All through dinner, while carrying on a highly political conversation with the Ambassador and interpreting for him with the Generalissimo, she was simultaneously concocting fudge on her chafing-dish. We all got some when dinner was over, and it was delicious. During dinner the Generalissimo sat in impassive near-silence; the attempts of Sir Arthur Blackburn, the Chinese Counsellor of the Embassy, to converse with him in Chinese (he allegedly knew no English) were defeated by the Generalissimo's thick Chekiang accent. He was an impressive figure, though, when after dinner, he withdrew and returned without his false teeth some of his impressiveness had gone. The only other person present was W. H. Donald, the Australian ex-journalist who lived permanently with the Chiangs and formed an invaluable link between them and the non-Chinese world. Donald was a curious man. Though he passed most of his life in China he never learnt a word of Chinese. Though he lived at the centre of a net of intrigues he was himself perfectly straightforward. Though almost everyone at court (except the Chiangs themselves) was financially corrupt, Donald was known to be disinterested and died a poor man. I used to go for occasional walks with him over the hills around Chungking. Conversation with him should have been more interesting than it was. He was inclined to hold forth, in a series of clichés, without ever saying anything very much. But one could see how useful he must be to Madame and to the Generalissimo, and his value to those of the foreign community whom he was willing to see was inestimable.

Air-raid alarms (the Chinese name for them was jing-bao, such a good word) were frequent at that time in Chungking. If one had to be bombed, Chungking was a good place for it. There were two kinds of alarm. The first went when the Japanese bombers, which had to fly a very long distance over country covered by the Chinese early-warning system, were two hours flying time away. When this one went one stayed within range of a shelter until the all-clear sounded, meaning the bombers were aiming elsewhere, or until the second alarm announced that the raid was on the Chungking area. No bombs fell on Chungking while I was there, but there were several second alarms. When that went, if it was day we would lay out immense flags on the consular lawns (in spite of which the Consul-General's house was entirely destroyed by a Japanese bomb soon after I left Chungking); if it was night all the lights would be turned off at the main (otherwise there was no black-out) and after watching the lights fading all over the town and in the villages across the river we would enter the dark tunnel in the rock, crowded with Chinese employees of the Mission, sitting there by candle-light until quite soon the all-clear went and the Japanese bombers started their long flight back to their bases. As autumn came on heavy mist settled permanently down over Chungking (it was a local saying that if the sun shone in Chungking in winter all the dogs barked). This diminished the danger of raids, and as the Hong Kong doctors had cleared her Iris flew up to Chungking on November 18th, a few days after the Ambassador had left me in charge of the Mission.

We stayed there till the New Year, and this proved a very happy time. I was for the first time in my life in charge of a more or less independent mission, dealing directly with the government of a major Power. We established ourselves in the Vice-Consul's house, which by judicious local purchases we made very attractive. There were occasional alarms but no air-raids. We lived entirely on Chinese food when alone, but were soon giving elaborate dinner-parties, in a more European style, though now the guests were principally Chinese, Ministers and government officials and other political figures, with a sprinkling of diplomats and journalists. Though conditions were not easy in Chungking then, the Chinese officials retained at times an agreeably light touch. One day we met at lunch K. C. Wu, who had been

3

appointed Mayor of Chungking the day before, and asked him
where his office was. 'Haha, I don't know,' he replied gaily. With
another leading Chinese politician, then Deputy Minister of
Communications, we had an interesting conversation about
opium-smoking, to which he was mildly addicted. 'You Europeans,' he said, 'make too much fuss about opium. In modera-
tion, it does you no more harm than whisky and is not less
soothing and agreeable. If you overdo it of course it is bad for
you, just as too much whisky is. The only difference is that too
much whisky makes you aggressive and disagreeable, whereas
with too much opium you become simply milder and more
harmless.'

British relations with China were then, briefly, good; we were
at war with Germany as they were with Germany's ally, Japan,
and though the two wars were not yet connected this gave us
a fellow-feeling. It was not clear how deep this feeling went. I was
commenting on it to a representative of one of the British shipping firms who inhabited a solid villa on the South Bank: he
pointed out of the window to the steep flights of steps that ran
down to the river's edge from the old city across the Yangtse;
'I've seen friends of mine running down those steps and being
stoned to death by a mob,' he told me. I reflected that the behaviour towards the Chinese of some of his colleagues in Shanghai
and the coastal ports was not without its share of the blame for
Chinese xenophobia. But for the moment at any rate all was
peace and amity between the British and Chinese in Chungking.
I even negotiated a renewal of the lease of the British naval base
at Weihaiwei. We could move about the town and the countryside in freedom and at ease. We drove out along the Chengtu
road with a picnic, goose-pâté and hot Chinese wine in a thermos.
Or we took a sampan down to Brass Gong Gorge, the first gorge
below Chungking, not sensational like the great gorges lower
down near Ichang but impressive enough. Or we would go over
to lunch in the gunboat, full of bearded young officers, or with
friends over the hills on the South Bank, Iris riding a tough little
pony up the flights of stone steps that constitute mountain paths
in Szechwan or along narrow causeways between flooded rice
fields. As Christmas approached we bought a large gander which

stalked commandingly about the Vice-Consular garden, certain
that he owned the whole place; we felt sad when he had to be
killed for our Christmas dinner, to which we invited all the little
British colony north of the river. Soon after Christmas the Ambassador appeared again with the Counsellor, Philip Broadmead,
who was to replace me as head of the Diplomatic Mission, and
we returned to Shanghai feeling a little flat.

In Shanghai life seemed to have changed little. The war in
Europe had hardly disturbed the intense social life of the foreign
community. We ourselves withdrew from it as far as we could,
excusing ourselves on the grounds of Iris's condition. But as the
war in Europe ceased to be phoney the situation in the Far East
became more menacing. The British garrisons ashore were withdrawn and the Far East fleet was thinned out. The exposed position in which the British had long been in China became more
obvious, and though there was no panic a number of wives and
children left for safer places. Our daughter Teresa was born on
April 2nd, 1940. She was christened in Shanghai Cathedral on
April 31st and we gave an elaborate party to celebrate this, amid
the news of Dunkirk. Our own position seemed precarious. The
Embassy was accredited to a Chinese government which the
Japanese did not recognize, and it was far from certain that they
would accept us as having any diplomatic immunity if they
declared war on England and took over the International Settlement. Moreover we were not sure how much longer our un-
recognized Embassy would go on representing any recognizable
government at home. Brave noises were coming out of beleaguered
Britain, but from that distance it was not easy to judge how much
longer it could hold out. Writing to my mother at this time I said,
'The news is really awful these days, and we feel useless and
ashamed of ourselves out here. I expect a turn for the better every
day, but meanwhile it's a continuous feeling of being about to go
to the dentist or go up for the Foreign Office interview, something unpleasant hanging over you all the time. It must be much
worse in England, here even now if you didn't read the papers
you wouldn't know there was a war on.' But of course we did
read the papers, we knew there was a war on, and it seemed to be
going very badly. In Shanghai we were surrounded by White

Russians and could easily visualize ourselves becoming White British, after the collapse of our country, in a situation no less precarious. As an indication of how out of touch we were, I recall myself saying to Gerald Tyrrell, as we stood on the balcony of his flat looking out over Shanghai's murmurous alleys one evening after the fall of Neville Chamberlain, 'Well, one good thing at least, this must mean the end of the Conservative Party.' I had underrated the resilience of that organization, its capacity to survive disgrace and humiliation. We wondered whether Iris and Teresa should go off to join Cecil Griffin in India, or perhaps take refuge with some distant Hayter cousins in New Zealand. But we kept putting off any decision; we gradually came to realize that the brave noises from England reflected the real situation there and we settled down to enjoy Teresa and wait to see what turned up.

What turned up as far as we were concerned was a telegram at the end of November telling me to proceed as soon as possible to London, to a post in the Far Eastern Department of the Foreign Office. This was very much what I wanted in many ways, but it posed other problems. The Blitz was on, and we read of children being evacuated to Canada and the United States; would it seem sensible to people in England to arrive there with an eight-months old baby? No one could tell us what we ought to think about this, but while we were still deliberating another telegram changed our destination to the Washington Embassy.

The next question was how to get there. We booked a passage in a C.P.R. liner but she was requisitioned at the last minute. The choice was then between two luxurious double cabins in a large, modern Japanese liner and one little cabin in a small, elderly American ship, with Teresa's nurse sleeping in a dormitory below decks. Though it was bad luck on the nurse we unhesitatingly chose the latter; the idea of escaping Japanese clutches in Shanghai, only to fall into their hands in a Japanese ship, was too unattractive. Something similar happened to a friend of ours a year later. He had sailed for the United States in a Japanese liner due to reach San Francisco early in December 1941; within sight of the west coast of America it inexplicably turned round and sailed back to Japan, arriving there after Pearl Harbor, and our friend went straight into an internment camp. This was exactly what we feared for ourselves, prematurely as it turned out.

We left Shanghai without regrets, though not without anxiety for our friends there, most of whom were in fact interned when the Japanese seized the Settlement a year later. But Washington seemed likely to provide more interesting work, nearer to the central problems of the war and still splendidly safe for Iris and Teresa.

As we crossed the Pacific we heard the news of the death of Lord Lothian, on whose staff in Washington I was supposed to be going to serve, but whom I had never met. The ship's wireless thereafter reported fantastic (but as it turned out not all unfounded) rumours about possible successors to the Washington Embassy; Lloyd George, for instance, or the Duke of Windsor. It was something of a relief to learn that it was to be Lord Halifax. He had long been a friend of Iris's family, and I had had some contact with him in my Geneva days.

Arriving by sea at San Francisco is undoubtedly the best way to enter the United States. You first see, or at any rate in those days you saw, a green, hilly and apparently uninhabited, harbourless coast (Drake sailed all the way up and down the California shore without discovering the entrance to San Francisco Bay). As you steam towards these green hills an opening suddenly appears, across it a magnificent high suspension bridge, and below the bridge, in the distance, a tall-towered city on what looks like a hilly island in an inland sea. This is San Francisco as seen through the Golden Gate. As a dramatic effect it far surpasses the sea approach to New York, splendid though this is, and of course the airport entries we are now accustomed to are totally inferior to either.

There is a further advantage for the European in making his first arrival in San Francisco, and that is that he normally proceeds at once to cross the continent. The European arriving by New York thinks, when he penetrates as far as Chicago, that he is half-way to the West Coast; if he arrives by San Francisco he has the impression that Chicago is practically on the East Coast, particularly if he makes the crossing, as we did, by train. An impression of the immensity of the country, and of the relative insignificance of the East Coast, is a lesson which a European cannot learn too early.

We arrived in Washington on the eve of Roosevelt's Third Inauguration, with the last year of America's neutrality lying ahead. Discordant voices, never rare in the United States, were rising to a violent pitch under the pressure of conflicting tensions, fear of 'foreign entanglement' in yet another European war on the one hand, and on the other, as President Conant put it at a Harvard Commencement I attended that summer, a feeling that America was letting others fight her battles for her. This led to crises of conscience which often resolved themselves in abuse of the British, seen either as trying to drag Americans into their war or alternatively as not fighting their own war hard enough or efficiently enough. Though Britain had many good and generous friends in America then, these tensions made the Embassy's position a difficult one, and Lord Halifax, soon after his arrival, found himself being pelted with eggs and tomatoes (on which he commented that America was a lucky country to have enough eggs and tomatoes to spare for throwing at Ambassadors).

Halifax was a complex and interesting character. Among many Americans he was at first unpopular because he was thought to be tarred with the appeasement brush, though he was hardly more involved in the actual appeasement of Germany than his universally popular predecessor Lord Lothian. But his natural tendency was in fact towards appeasement, and this was sometimes a good thing, sometimes not. As Viceroy of India he had appeased Gandhi, and this was good. As a member of the Chamberlain government he had appeased the Nazis, and this was bad. As British Ambassador in Washington he appeased the Americans, and this was, in the circumstances, good. He was a man of great ability and subtlety, with considerable charm when he chose to exercise it, which was intermittently. He was not exactly energetic, but his abilities and his inherited privileges carried him naturally and easily to the highest situations. He nearly became Prime Minister instead of Churchill when Chamberlain fell; if he had he might well have concluded that there was no prospect of a British victory, with disastrous consequences to the world. He was a great believer in privilege, his own included; it was not always easy to know what else he believed in, though his religious convictions were unquestionably strong. He had some Stoic virtues. Iris and I were due to lunch at the Embassy the day the news came of his second son's death at El Alamein. We assumed the lunch would be cancelled but it was not, and he and Lady Halifax, whom we all admired unreservedly, were almost unendurably brave. Whatever his failings in other situations, he did in the end become a great ambassador, in what is perhaps the most difficult diplomatic post in the world. He lived down his initial unpopularity, and by the end of his time in America he was widely admired and respected.

The Embassy over which he presided was a very different affair from Clark Kerr's rather ramshackle little empire in China. Housed in Lutyens's handsome palazzo on Massachusetts Avenue, it was nearly two hundred strong, not counting wives, when we arrived, and by the time we left, three and a half years later, the number of British officials in Washington had reached five figures. The Ambassador presided as a kind of Cabinet Minister over this overseas Whitehall, keeping it in some kind of coherent order by the force of his political status (he was still nominally a member of the War Cabinet) and by his un-selfconscious assumption of effortless superiority. The Embassy's role was not unlike that of the Cabinet Secretariat in London. It grew rapidly in size; at the end of my time in Washington there were, under the Ambassador, seven Ministers, twelve Counsellors and innumerable First Secretaries (of whom I was one) besides shoals of lesser fry. Outside all this, but loosely controlled by the Ambassador, were numerous special missions, military and civil; at that time every Whitehall department needed, or at any rate wished, to have its own representation in Washington.

Within this huge organization my own role was necessarily a very minor one. The Chancery of the Embassy, in which I had the second place and of which I was for a time the acting head, was in a sense the core of the whole great apple, so that I was not entirely without responsibilities. The job was a desk job. Many were the dire warnings uttered, before we went to the States, about the heavy pressures of Washington hospitality on secretaries at the British Embassy. But these warnings related to the days before the war and the vast expansion of British officialdom in Washington. Now, not only was the Embassy itself enormous, so that no one below the rank of Minister was worth the attention of a Washington hostess, but there were also special missions, full of Field Marshals, Admirals and even Dukes. So we did not find Washington hostesses exactly competing for our favours (though Mrs. Truxtun Beale, perhaps the most distinguished and elegant of them all, was very kind to us). We did not regret this relative obscurity. We made many friends at less exalted levels, and the pressure of work meant that freedom from heavy social activity was a boon. But some there was; Iris's diary, a month or two after our arrival, records that 'William and I had a rather depressing argument about the futility of life here and the contrast between it and life in England.' I cannot now remember why we argued, and am surprised that we should have, since we were in basic agreement on this subject; but this entry in the diary is at least an indication of how we were feeling.

Our Washington existence was in fact full and busy, but not particularly interesting to anyone but ourselves. There were one or two highlights. Owing to my recent service in China I was masquerading as the Embassy's Far Eastern expert, and this led to some involvement in the negotiations which the United States Government was conducting with the Japanese in the summer of 1941. The Americans were then beginning to bring heavy pressure on the Japanese economy, in the hope of slowing down Japan's pressure on China. The British Government, while generally sympathetic with this policy, was a little nervous about its impact on our Far Eastern interests, and indulged in some back-seat driving. We were afraid that the Japanese, if pressed too hard by the Americans, might turn south and seize our possessions in South-East Asia, to ensure the supplies of raw materials of which American pressure was threatening to deprive them. In November and early December 1941 a Japanese mission was in Washington negotiating with the State Department, and London was watching these negotiations with some alarm. On the morning of Sunday, December 7th, the Ambassador sent me down to the White House with the latest of a series of messages from London about all this. When I got back to the Embassy he told me he was going riding that afternoon, and asked what I meant to do. I said we were going to take the car out into the country and go for a walk. After lunch, just as we were due to start, the Ambassador telephoned to say that the President had just rung him up and told him the Japanese were bombing Pearl Harbor. This seemed to me an improbable story; we had always thought they were much more likely to go for Hong Kong and Singapore, leaving the American possessions in the Pacific alone, at first at any rate. So I asked Lord Halifax if he was sure he'd got it right. 'The Pwesident', (that was how he pronounced the letter R,) 'the Pwesident *said* Pearl Harbor', he repeated, a little plaintively. He asked what I thought we should do next, and I said he should ask the Embassy telephone operator to put in a call to London; I would then come round to the Embassy and take it. In due course I got through to a rather somnolent-sounding Resident Clerk at the Foreign Office and conveyed this interesting piece of news to him, with the request that he pass it to the Prime Minister. 'What was that place?' he asked, 'could you spell it?' He did not seem at all sure that the Prime Minister would be interested. So far as I know this was how the news of Pearl Harbor first reached London.

The sensation created in Washington was of course rather stronger. At first it seemed to take the shape of panic. The whole Pacific Fleet, we were told, had been sunk, the Atlantic Fleet could not get through the Panama Canal, and there was nothing to prevent the Japanese landing on the West Coast wherever and whenever they liked (and presumably marching on Washington). The disorder and confusion in the capital were palpable. It is a remarkable example of America's untidy efficiency that within a few months of this humiliating disaster this disordered, confused capital had directed the construction of the largest and most powerful fleet the world had ever seen and had begun the inexorable process of crushing Japanese imperialism.

But all this was some way off. Meanwhile America's discordant voices were as strong as ever. There was a joke current in Washington then about the different wars that were being fought, in order of importance. Easily first was the war against the President. Then came the war against the British. In third place was the war

3*

against Japan. The war against Germany, which had been impru-
dent enough to declare war on the United States in the wake of
Pearl Harbor, came if I remember rightly seventh; I forgot
which internal battles came fourth, fifth and sixth. The war
proper took people in differing ways. One Senator's wife, on
whom Iris had called, in accordance with Washington protocol,
after meeting her at lunch with the Halifaxes, sent a note saying,
'Will call back when the war is over'. But by and large the war
made little or no difference to social life. Petrol was rationed, and
later meat, but both lavishly, and every other article, other than
those habitually imported from Europe, was available in the usual
American abundance. Chilean and South African wines replaced
those from France and Germany, American wines enjoyed a
brief domestic popularity, caviar was in short supply, otherwise
tables groaned as before.

My own work increased in intensity. I found myself involved
in Anglo-American planning for the civil affairs of various
countries we were hoping to occupy. This was carried on in the
Pentagon, under the Chairmanship of an American General
whose booming voice drowned all opposition; one of the British
team's main duties was to keep the State Department on speaking
terms with the American military authorities. The affairs of Italy
preoccupied us most, and here we evolved an institution called
Allied Military Government of Occupied Territories, or AMGOT
for short. The shortened version had to be officially abandoned,
not, as was rumoured, because it had an obscene connotation in
Turkish but because Secretary Morgenthau thought it too remi-
niscent of other sinister acronyms such as OGPU or GESTAPO.
However, it persisted in popular use and led to one of the neatest
jokes of the Second World War. The Rodd family, owing to
their Italian connexions, were much involved in Allied Military
Government in Italy, and when it was wound up the process
was described as Amgötterdämmerung, or the Twilight of the
Rodds.

Civil Affairs planning was one of the sectors of the war effort
in which I was, inevitably, admitted to deep secrets. There were
others from which I was of course excluded, among them the
preparations for atomic warfare. Lord Waverley, then in charge

of the British atomic programme, came to Washington in 1943 to discuss it with the highest American authorities and was disconcerted and offended to find that not only the President but the British Ambassador were away. Ronnie Campbell, the Minister, asked me to help keep him happy at dinner at a Washington hotel. But it was a glum and unhappy meal. Waverley could not discuss his business in my presence, or indeed at all in a public restaurant, and sat in grim silence, while Ronnie and I talked feverishly across him. Things were not made easier by the mocking presence at a neighbouring table of Isaiah Berlin and John Russell. Other visitors were less disconcerting. Isaiah brought Chaim Weizmann to see me, the only incontestably great man I have ever met. Another caller was the Archduke Otto, then claimant to the Habsburg throne (his staff referred to him as 'His Majesty'). Washington was the centre for all those who wanted to reconstruct the world after the war, and most of them would call at the British Embassy. Isaiah or I, for some reason, usually saw them. Isaiah was then writing his famous series of reports on the American internal scene, which aroused so much interest in London. They would come through me on their way up to the Ambassador for final approval. They contained extraordinary facts about the inmost workings of the United States Government. I would say to Isaiah, 'All this is very interesting, but where did you get it from? What is your evidence? Is it really true?' 'It is true,' Isaiah would reply, 'at a deeper level.' I would then pass it on up unaltered to the Ambassador.

Life in Washington, though busy, was not disagreeable. We lived for our first two years in a little box-like house on Woodley Road, near the Episcopalian Cathedral. Turned out of that, we moved to an even smaller house in Georgetown. This is the most fashionable sector of Washington, but it is very hot in summer, and was then at any rate very dirty; one summer I had to move out and have the house fumigated, so infested was it with fleas. The Washington summer climate, in those pre-air-conditioning days, was pretty intolerable, and Iris and Teresa would go north for a month or two; I joined them briefly when I could. But though I was aware that what I was doing was on the whole useful we began to feel it intolerable to spend the whole war in comfort and security outside England, and I agitated for a return to the Foreign Office. Talking it over with Iris one evening I said to her, 'It's all very well to ask for a transfer to the Office, but suppose it turns out to be something dreary like No. 2 in the General Department?' This was precisely the post to which I learnt, a few days later, that I had been appointed. This was, I think, the only occasion during my diplomatic career when I asked for a transfer; the result showed how unprofitable such requests usually are.

We left Washington in May 1944. We had to spend several days in New York waiting for a ship, one of them in the company of Donald Maclean who was to succeed me in Washington. Iris and I had both known him for many years, but apparently not well. He seemed to us both to be a typically successful Foreign Office type, agreeable, good-looking, with a particularly pleasant soft voice, holding rather conventional views and showing an occasional touch of arrogance. We were quite unaware of his Bohemian outbreaks, let alone, of course, of his long service as a Soviet spy. I seem to have had a fairly extensive acquaintance among detected Soviet spies. Guy Burgess I knew slightly when he was working for Hector McNeil in the Foreign Office; I never felt the charm he clearly had for so many people. Kim Philby I met once in the room of the then head of the Secret Service, who introduced him as 'one of our most promising young men'; I can only remember an agreeable, brown-faced, smiling presence. John Vassall was on my staff when I was Ambassador in Moscow. No characteristics common to all four are obvious. Detecting spies cannot be easy. Certainly no such idea crossed my mind that spring in New York, as I discussed with Donald Maclean the work he would be taking over in Washington, and tried to arrange for him to move into our house in Georgetown.

We set sail on May 11th in a British ship carrying American troops as reinforcements for the forthcoming invasion of Europe. We were in a large slow convoy, and the crossing took fourteen days, undisturbed by any submarine alarms. Teresa, aged four, was the only child on board and was much admired by all; on one occasion she was asked to dine (without us) in the officers' mess. But her newly acquired and often repeated accomplishment of counting up to twelve was too much for a seasick

American soldier in the next cabin; 'For Gawd's sake,' he cried, 'can't someone teach that kid thirteen?'

We arrived safely at Liverpool on May 24th, and after a few days with Iris's parents at Stalybridge I left her and Teresa there and set off for London and the Foreign Office.

FIVE

A Promising Career

Service in the Washington Embassy, if performed with reasonable credit, was in those days considered a passport to a successful future career. It was, therefore, as I have suggested in the last chapter, rather disconcerting to find myself appointed to the General Department, even though I had to some extent brought it on myself by my repeated requests to be transferred to London before the war ended. The General Department was a kind of waste-paper basket into which questions not interesting to the more central departments of the Foreign Office were then thrust. These were mainly questions like civil aviation, inland transport or oil, of great importance in themselves but primarily the responsibility of other Whitehall ministries, the Foreign Office being only involved in arranging the mechanics of negotiations to be carried on by others and in seeing that too many foreign toes were not trodden upon. General Department questions were for the most part outside the purview of the Office's more influential members and were regarded by them as a nuisance; their main preoccupation at this time was the preparation of the post-war settlements, and the members of General Department were not within what Sir Ivone Kirkpatrick's memoirs describe as 'the Inner Circle'.

My service in this waste-paper basket was not of long duration, though my emergence from it was due not to any merit of my own but to a major disaster to the Office and the Service. On February 1st, 1945, one of the aircraft carrying part of the delegation to the Yalta Conference crashed into the sea near Malta. Among those killed were Peter Loxley, perhaps the most promising Foreign Office man of his generation and quite certain, if he had lived, to have become Permanent Under-Secretary, and

Armine Dew whom I knew less well and who was then No. 2 in the Southern Department. I was appointed to succeed Dew, not without some protest from the Under-Secretary in charge of the General Department who quoted promises made to him by the personnel people that 'a strong General Department' would be built up, and who regarded my sideways transfer as in conflict with these promises, although in fact he had not shown any great enthusiasm for my services while I was under his supervision. Sorry as I was to step into a dead man's shoes I was delighted by this transfer. The Southern Department dealt primarily with the affairs of South-East Europe, primarily the Balkans, primarily Greece; these were then particularly active and involved the direct attention of Foreign Office ministers and leading officials. I was back in 'the Inner Circle'.

Our domestic arrangements began to improve, too, at about this time. When we first returned to England in May 1944 it did not seem wise for Iris and Teresa to come to London. The flying-bomb season soon began, and life in the country was clearly more sensible for them, so I took a room in the flat where my sister Alethea was living. But as the summer wore on it appeared to me (wrongly as it turned out) that a German defeat before Christmas was inevitable, and I thought that if we waited till then London houses would become more expensive and more difficult to find. So after some searching we found a nice little house in St. Leonard's Terrace, a typical London house, on five floors, with about one room on each floor, but with a pleasant southwards view across Burton Court to Chelsea Hospital. We moved in on January 1st, 1945, with all our possessions. Two days later a V2 rocket fell on Chelsea Hospital. It blew in every window in the front of our house and brought down most of the ceilings. We wondered whether we could stay. But in those days blitzed houses left empty were usually looted, and as the kitchen and one little bed-room and one bathroom, at the back of the house, had all retained their ceilings and their glass we decided to stick it out. It was very uncomfortable at first, but the first-aid repair was swift and effective and the house gradually became habitable again, though the blast had left aching gaps between walls and window-frames through which whistled the cold winds of that harsh winter. In the end these were closed too, and as the war drew to a close we started off on our usual round of social entertaining, hampered though we were by shortages of all kinds. The hardships involved, such as they were, were suffered more by Iris than by me. Not only was I in a relatively comfortable office all day, but once my transfer to the Southern Department had taken place, I began to travel. In July of that year I went to the Potsdam Conference not only to represent the Southern Department's interests but as Secretary of the British delegation. This was the only time I really felt that we had won the war. This impression was less vivid at the Victory Parade in the Tiergarten than in the so-called 'No. 1 mess', looted German wine in a handsome requisitioned villa. It was most vivid of all at the R.A.F. concert in the Neues Schloss. For some reason that evening the world seemed to belong to us. We drove by twilight along the dusty alleys of the park, the fountains playing. The concert was in a candle-lit room on the ground floor of the palace. In the intervals we walked out on to the terrace. Mr. Attlee was there. No one could be bothered to talk to him, and I condescendingly introduced him to minor members of the United States delegation. A few days later he was Prime Minister.

Berlin, which we visited once or twice, looked like a preview of the collapse of civilization, assuming that collapse to have occurred in a pre-atomic age. The streets were lined with immense, tottering, cracked façades; clearly they would all have to come down, but who would clear away the rubble? In a kind of sandy waste in front of the ruined Reichstag desperate-looking Berliners were selling watches and silk underclothes to slovenly, bronzed Soviet soldiers, mainly Asiatics. A few steps down the entrances to the underground stations was a level of filthy water, with nameless objects half submerged. Outside the semi-ruined Reichskanzlei a Russian sentry tipped up a felt boot, and out poured Iron Crosses and other German decorations; we helped ourselves. Inside the building steady souvenir-hunting was going on, though no one had yet thought of taking the seat of Hitler's private lavatory. Our R.A.S.C. driver picked up an immense chunk of the brownish marble top of Hitler's desk and dropped it on to the granite floor so that it broke up into more portable fragments. This was twelve years after the foundation of the *tausendjähriges Reich*.

Enough has been written about the Conference itself. To me the most memorable incident occurred during a debate on Bulgaria. Churchill had been denouncing that wretched little country in a long, rumbling speech—'crouching in the Balkans, fawning on Germany', and saying she must be punished. Stalin when he came to reply used his favourite technique of short sentences interrupted by pauses for interpretation. 'I do not,' he said, 'wish to give my colleagues a lesson on policy' (Pause). 'But if I may say so I do not think policy should be based on considerations of revenge' (Pause, during which we wondered what he would say it should be based on; justice, the interests of the masses, the preservation of peace?) 'In my opinion,' he went on, 'policy should be based on the calculation of forces.' One had always known it, but it was interesting to hear it from the horse's mouth.

Stalin was dressed like the Emperor of Austria in a bad musical comedy; cream jacket with gold-braided collar, blue trousers with a red stripe and one jewelled order. Generally he affected an impassive, benign, dignified demeanour, but once when trying to sell some idea to us he suddenly fell into the gestures of an Armenian carpet-seller, shoulders shrugging rapidly up and down and hands spread out. His wicked side emerged too. Maisky, until shortly before Soviet Ambassador in London, came into the Conference room one day and was warmly, too warmly, greeted by Churchill and Eden; Stalin turned a cold, basilisk glare on him and he was never seen again by Western eyes until many years later, after Stalin's death, I myself recognized him in the Bolshoi theatre in Moscow, where I was by then Ambassador.

Truman was perky, precise and very definite in his manner. Personally very modest, he clearly had the self-confidence inspired by the immense force which he represented, a force immeasurably increased during that very meeting by the Los Alamos explosion.

Churchill was tired and below his form. He also suffered from the belief that he knew everything and need not read briefs. Stalin was almost always late for meetings, and we spent long periods in the waiting-room allotted to the British delegation, which happened to be the Crown Prince's library. This would have been a good time to read briefs, but instead he and the Foreign Secretary read the Crown Prince's books and exchanged jokes about the comic dedications 'to darling little Willy from his loving Great-grandmother Victoria R.I.', that sort of thing. When we got into the meetings Stalin and Molotov, always very well briefed, would put pointed questions. 'What's the answer to that?' the Prime Minister would say, turning round with difficulty to his advisers seated behind him. We could not say, 'If you had read our brief you would know', and tried in low mutters which he could not catch to explain the genesis of the Tito-Subasic agreement or what had happened to King Michael of Roumania. When the Conservative Government fell and Churchill and Eden were replaced by Attlee and Bevin the British delegation became much more business-like. The new Ministers, less experienced in foreign affairs and therefore less confident that they had all the facts at their fingertips, held daily meetings with their advisers, asked what questions were likely to come up during the day and read the briefs giving the answers.

This was the first contact most of us had had with Bevin. We were all immensely impressed. He radiated determination and personal force. What was less obvious was that this heavy, ugly man had extraordinary charm; all the Foreign Office delegation were captivated before they knew what was happening. From the first Attlee left almost all the conduct of the negotiations to him, and he waded in with a self-confidence and skill that took everyone by surprise. He did wonders, and it was not his fault that by the end of the meeting that euphoric feeling we had had at the start was beginning to fade under the first blasts of the Cold War. Attlee, at that stage, chiefly impressed us by his almost excessive modesty. Towards the end of the Conference I put it into our Delegation's head that it would be a graceful gesture if the Conference sent a message to Churchill and Eden, absent since their fall from power, thanking them for their collaboration. Attlee adopted the idea with alacrity, and in putting it to the Conference talked of sending a message to 'the *Prime Minister* and Mr. Eden'.

Shortly after my return from Potsdam I became head of the Southern Department, and in that capacity I began to see more

and more of Bevin as the affairs of Greece began to take up more
and more of his time. He was substantially the ablest and most
powerful Foreign Secretary of my time. I remember once
praising him to Douglas Jay, who while agreeing generally said
that his lack of any formal education handicapped him. I saw
what Douglas meant. There was a certain confusion in his
thought processes on occasion, and some *naïveté*, which a University education might perhaps have sorted out. I remember listening with astonishment to a conversation between him and Hector
McNeil, when we were discussing aid to Greece in preparation
for a forthcoming visit there, in which they considered quite
seriously the advantages of supplying Greek women with clogs.
Bevin read a lot, and constantly came across words which he had
never heard pronounced, and which he in due course produced
with rather idiosyncratic pronunciations of his own; 'clitch' for
cliché, for instance, and 'fackaid' for façade.

But these were minor blemishes. In general he was, as I have
said, the finest Foreign Secretary I encountered. He was a good
listener and an absorptive reader, but he was his own man and
made up his own mind. His critics sometimes attributed his almost
notorious popularity with the permanent officials of the Foreign
Office to a belief that they had captured him, that they could
always persuade him to follow their recommendations. Nothing
could be further from the truth. He would listen patiently to
what we had to say, but he was liable to ask penetrating questions
and his decisions were often not those we expected or wanted.
He could be quite critical, too; once when Rex Leeper, on leave
from Athens, was expounding to him his views on Greek politics
he said scornfully, 'You sound to me like 'Erb Morrison trying to
fix an election.' The reasons why we liked him were different.
First, he was a good boss. Though he could be severe and even
ruthless to his officials in private, he supported them publicly and
defended their interests. Then, he was powerful in Cabinet. We
knew that if we could reach an agreement with him on what
needed to be done it would be done. Attlee left him a very free
hand in foreign affairs, and once when someone murmured to
him that what we wanted to do might not be welcome to the
Chancellor of the Exchequer he commented, 'I'll swing that

Dalton round my 'ead.' Finally, and contrary to general belief, the Foreign Office likes a Foreign Secretary who has a mind of his own and takes his own decisions, and this was what Bevin was like. So a great bond of mutual respect and, indeed, affection united him and his staff, to a degree unparalleled in my experience.

His main political coadjutor in the Office in my time was Hector McNeil, the Parliamentary Under-Secretary. McNeil, whose early death left a gap in the Labour Party which no one else has adequately filled, resembled Bevin in combining a certain *naïveté* with a great deal of natural shrewdness (though it was not perhaps very shrewd of him to have introduced Guy Burgess first into his private office and then into the Foreign Service). He was a nice, cheerful, efficient Scot, a former journalist in the Beaverbrook press, who soon settled down into a very capable junior minister. We set off for Greece together on November 12th, 1945. The Embassy Daimler met us at the airport. I was on the tip seat. When we drew up outside the Embassy the sergeant-driver, as I was pulling myself out of the car, slammed the door on my right hand and stood smartly at the salute. Released after a bit, I walked up the Embassy's marble steps dripping blood and was efficiently bandaged by Primrose Leeper. We immediately set off on a protracted series of talks with Greek political leaders, interspersed with banquets and receptions.

Greece was then in a very bad way. Soon after its liberation from German occupation civil war had broken out; the British Embassy had been under siege and was still spattered with the marks of rifle bullets. This first attempt of the Greek communists to seize power had been defeated, with British help; the second and more serious one lay in the future. Meanwhile the British Government, with very inadequate resources and itself under appalling financial and economic strains, was struggling to build up the non-Communist forces in the country, which they believed with good reason to represent a substantial majority of the population. But the leaders of these forces were not very effective; they were divided among themselves and lacked any real capacity for organizing the Greek state, which as a result of the Nazi occupation had more or less collapsed, or for re-establishing its shattered economy. The non-issue, or so it seemed to us, about whether Greece should be a monarchy or a republic occupied a disproportionate amount of their attention and prevented them from working together. McNeil and I and Rex Leeper, the Ambassador, would sit for hours listening to their interminable monologues, full of impracticable proposals and complaints against each other. The only pleasurable occasion during these negotiations was a moment after dinner with some left-wing Greek politicians when McNeil, in a relaxed mood, asked our hosts what the Greek national sport was. Without a moment's pause for consideration they all replied in chorus 'politics'.

By this time my injured hand was beginning to throb unbearably; I had to hold it up throughout these endless meetings and could hardly sleep at night. Eventually we patched up some sort of a government and McNeil returned to London, while I went off to the British Military Hospital where my hand, which had now gone septic, needed urgent attention. This accident proved a blessing in disguise, though it did not seem so to poor Iris, whom I had foolishly sought to reassure by telling her that I was being given penicillin. This had exactly the opposite effect. In those days penicillin, though in lavish supply to the armed forces, was only obtainable by civilians if they were on the point of death, and the news that I was being treated with it made Iris fear the worst. She could get no news from the Foreign Office and had a bag packed ready to fly at any moment to my death-bed in Athens. But actually, after two small operations, my hand was making a rapid recovery, and I was soon able to leave the hospital to convalesce under the Leepers' hospitable roof. As a result I saw much more of Greece than if I had returned to London with Hector McNeil. Almost my first outing was a little walk round the tiny Byzantine churches on Mount Hymettus with Osbert Lancaster, then living in the Embassy and working as its Press Attaché, and we had agreeable expeditions later to the Peloponnese and the Gulf of Corinth.

I returned to London on December 12th just in time to set off for Moscow and the Foreign Ministers' Conference (Bevin, Byrnes, Molotov). I flew out in Bevin's plane. We spent the night in Berlin and were due to start on again at seven next morning. I overslept, and when I got to the aircraft the whole party were in their seats and waiting. The Foreign Secretary, a magnanimous man, contented himself with saying 'Good afternoon'. Moscow, when we reached it after a hazardous flight through a snowstorm, made a curious impression. Unlike Berlin and London it was undamaged by bombing. In fact it was almost unchanged outwardly and even inwardly since I left it two years before the war. Every other European capital had been more profoundly affected by the War, it seemed, than Moscow; there the same few men, in the same fantastic palace, still ruled over the same silent, undernourished, overcrowded masses. The delegation's office was in the familiar white ballroom of the Embassy, looking across at the domes and pinnacles of the Kremlin. Jack Ward and I shared one of the familiar, fusty, over-decorated bedrooms in the National Hotel, and were served with the familiar, over-elaborate breakfast of cold coffee, cold fried eggs, caviar and vodka. It was like coming back to an unloved home. The Conference achieved nothing. Byrnes entitles his chapter on it 'Moscow Ends an Impasse'. This was over-optimistic. Byrnes himself was very active, in a way which excited the profoundest distrust of the British delegation. I can remember a moment when, at the Bolshoi, Bevin gave the clenched-fist salute of comradely solidarity in reply to the audience's applause. But it was then the American Secretary of State who was making all the concessions. They were in vain, and the results of the Conference were so negligible that one can hardly say that history would have been any different had it never occurred.

I was not travelling all the time, however. There was a great deal of work to do in London, mainly concerned with Greece. In the course of it I evolved a proposal, which got quite a long way but was ultimately abortive, to hand over Cyprus to Greece. I regard this as one of the more painful missed opportunities of the post-war period. It would have been a gesture, like Gladstone's cession of the Ionian Islands, that would have endeared us for ever to the Greeks, one of the few countries in Europe that in the past has genuinely liked us and with whom we were at that time very popular, though the Cyprus question later soured our relationship, probably for good. Moreover I believe the surrender of Cyprus to Greece might well have been popular in England.

The Greek war record, though patchy, had had some heroic passages. The Turks, on the other hand, had come badly out of the war in popular esteem, only joining the allies when their victory was certain. They would no doubt have protested, but their protests could have been ignored, and as they were then under strong pressure from the Soviet Union over the Dardanelles and their eastern provinces they were in no position to forfeit Western goodwill by being intransigent about Cyprus, as they were able to be with impunity when the problems of the island became acute some years later.

I knew that this proposal would be unpopular in the Colonial Office and the Service Departments, and thought I could meet their criticisms by saying that I was sure that if we handed over Cyprus we could count on the Greeks giving us all the strategic facilities we needed, both in the island and elsewhere on Greek territory. To the argument that such facilities were much less valuable than sovereign control I returned an argument based on my experience at the Washington Embassy dealing with the terms of the American leased bases in the British West Indies. The Colonial Office had then argued that the terms of these leases involved an effective transfer to the United States of sovereignty over these British islands. Exactly similar leases could, I said, certainly be obtained by the British in Cyprus and, if needed, elsewhere in Greece as a condition of handing over Cyprus. But these arguments were brushed aside by the Service Departments, and the Colonial Office added the additional point that if we gave up Cyprus we might conceivably find ourselves obliged sooner or later to surrender sovereignty over some other British colony. Bevin, who had given the idea some slightly tepid support, then decided to let sleeping dogs lie. This was perhaps not surprising in the circumstances. The Service Departments still, in the aftermath of the war, carried great weight, and the Colonial Office could perhaps not be expected, in 1946, to foresee how silly their attitude would look as little as ten years later. Still, if I had got my way, many young Englishmen, Greeks and Turks now dead would be alive.

One of the advantages of becoming head of the Southern Department was that it brought me into closer touch with Sir

Orme Sargent, universally known as Moley. Indeed, in the room
I now occupied, a little trap high up in the wall would often fly
open and Moley's long, lizard-like head would protrude through
it from his office next door, smiling derisively and asking some
unanswerable question. He was then Deputy Under-Secretary
(Political), a post I was to fill myself some years later, and the
Southern Department was under his supervision. He was a fine
specimen of the pre-First World War Foreign Office clerk, dating
from the days when the Foreign Office and the Diplomatic Service were separate services. It was widely, though erroneously,
believed that he had never crossed the Channel, and certainly his
whole career had been spent in London. He was a bachelor, and
lived in the Conservative Club, continuing his residence there
under a Labour Government, a situation which Labour Ministers,
to their credit, accepted without question. He was a splendid man
to work for, demanding perhaps but lucid, quick and penetrating;
nothing ever needed to be explained to him, he understood what
you were trying to say before you could finish saying it. He had a
delightfully dry and caustic sense of humour which lightened and
enlightened all his official work. In February of 1946 he became
Permanent Under-Secretary in succession to Sir Alexander
Cadogan, and in August of that same year, at his instance, I was
translated across the Office to become head of the Services Liaison
Department, a very special department which worked directly
under the Permanent Under-Secretary.

As its name implied the Services Liaison Department was
mainly concerned with injecting Foreign Office views into the
Service Departments. The head of the Department sat in with the
Joint Planners under the Chiefs of Staff, and dealt with all Intelligence questions. The resulting closer acquaintance with the
Intelligence organizations, while never entirely removing doubts
about the real value of their operations, inspired respect and liking
for the men engaged in them. Indeed contact with the Service
Departments as a whole produced in a civilian like myself a surprised appreciation of the high personal qualities of the Services,
at any rate at the centre. It was not entirely clear to me how far
this appreciation was reciprocated. The planners and the Intelligence chiefs, particularly the former, were inclined to feel that the

Foreign Office, while well enough organized for the tactical handling of events, had very little idea of strategy, of where it was going, and no machinery for working on this. I conveyed these feelings to my superiors in the Office, who reacted with some irritation, even suggesting that the Service planners should attach someone to the Foreign Office to see how it really worked. My comment on this was that the attached officer would find his worst fears confirmed; he would discover a large number of able and intelligent men working away like beavers to get off answers to telegrams, but that if he tried to find out how and where long-term policy was worked out he would be completely baffled. Eventually, the Office agreed, as an experiment, to create a small planning staff and attach it to the Service Liaison Department, which was renamed for the purpose the Permanent Under-Secretary's Department. With varying fortunes this little nucleus survives, now I believe somewhat expanded, until this day.

Another of the Service Department's complaints was that the Foreign Office's liaison with them was established at too lowly a level, that of Counsellor, the rank I then held. The Office solved that one neatly by giving me the personal rank of Assistant Under-Secretary, and I thus received a totally unmerited but welcome promotion and increase of salary. Altogether I was getting quite a lot out of my association with the Services. I went off on tours of inspection of the British intelligence organizations in Germany, the Far East and the Middle East, where I revisited Cairo for the first time since my childhood and did most of my business with Donald Maclean, dining *en famille* with him and Melinda in their nice house, a twin of my father's old house in Zamalek, a cosy conventional Foreign Office evening. I also visited Washington and Ottawa. I lectured at the Imperial Defence College. I attended a number of grand parties, among them one which I described in a letter to Iris in April 1949 as 'quite a day at Greenwich yesterday. I saw all the people we knew were going to be there and in addition Colin Anderson, Hugh Gaitskell who greeted me effusively (but I couldn't at first remember who he was), Monty who gave me a firm handshake and a nod, and the Duke of Gloucester with whom I had three minutes' embarrassing conversation about nothing. Admiral Vian asked after Priscilla and said he couldn't think why she didn't marry again. Mountbatten and the Duke of Edinburgh were there but I didn't talk to either of them, too bad. Tedder and Fraser of the North Cape were very genial. I had to address the party briefly and impromptu in defence of the Foreign Office, it went all right. Jack Slessor gave me a lift home.'

It was soon after this party that I began to hear rumours of an impending transfer. I had now been over five years at the Foreign Office, considerably more than the average spell in London, and I was beginning to hope that I might get a small independent post abroad, preferably somewhere fairly exotic like Damascus or Bangkok. So I was slightly disappointed to hear that my destiny was to be Minister at the Embassy in Paris, which was neither small nor an independent post nor exotic. Except for three not very enjoyable months there learning French I had never lived in Paris, I had few friends there, and I found the prospects of making my way in that formidable world somewhat daunting.

We arrived in Paris early in December 1949, and moved straight into a large, gloomy but commodious flat inherited from my predecessor Ashley Clarke. This flat was in the Seizième Arrondissement, the Kensington of Paris, a collection of uninteresting nineteenth-century streets but suitable for diplomatic habitation in a conventional way; in a play we saw in Paris a young man says to his sister who is behaving in a square manner, 'tu es affreusement Seizième ce soir'. But dull though it was the flat served us well and we spent all our three and a half Paris years in it.

The Ambassador during those years was Oliver Harvey. This was lucky for us. He knew Paris very well, having served there twice before, and his contacts were extensive. Moreover, unlike some Ambassadors with extensive contacts, he was generous in sharing them with his staff. Whenever he had interesting people in the Embassy we were invited to meet them. His way of entertaining was very different from that of his predecessors, Duff and Diana Cooper. They gave parties of a dazzling and indeed sometimes intimidating sophistication. This made the British Embassy the lodestar of Paris society in the immediate post-liberation period, but it was not perhaps the style best fitted to the kind of political world that took over the Fourth Republic when General de Gaulle withdrew to Colombey-les-deux-Eglises in 1946. The leaders of the political parties that shared power in that period, the Socialists, the M.R.P. (roughly speaking, Christian Democrats) and the Radical and Independent groups to the right of them, were for the most part men of intelligence and integrity, but they were socially somewhat insecure. They hardly felt at home in the blaze of the Cooper glamour. The Harveys suited them better. They were not intimidating. They were friends from before the war. They had the best chef in Paris. They had a fine collection of Post-Impressionist pictures. They preferred to entertain *en petit comité*. So Iris and I would often find ourselves lunching or dining at the Embassy in parties of six or eight, the other guests being Cabinet Ministers and their wives.

The Ambassador's generosity with his contacts was not his only merit as a chief. He was administratively efficient, tidy-minded and quick-working. He was punctilious and courteous in all his social obligations, which are very heavy for the British Ambassador in Paris. He was good at delegation, and left his staff, once they had his confidence, substantial latitude in their own fields. His views were emphatic and strongly held, often surprisingly radical, belying his mild and owlish appearance, but he did not impose them on his subordinates. His wife, a distant connexion of Iris's, was a woman of exceptional charm and distinction of appearance, and was as kind and helpful to us as he was.

He was at times criticized for having deprived the Embassy of the highly polished gloss it had previously held, particularly by some who had frequented it in the Coopers' time and were now excluded. This did not worry him unduly, and in fact from time to time brilliant entertainments occurred; I remember particularly one summer evening when the Marquis de Cuevas's ballet danced in the Embassy garden, one of the most enchanting and memorable evenings I have ever known. Also there were occasional large dinner parties to which the Paris 'monde' were invited. The 'monde' was the local equivalent, on a richer, grander and more sophisticated scale, of the Viennese 'erste Gesellschaft' I had frequented in my youth. It is the world so faithfully depicted in the

Paris novels of Miss Nancy Mitford, the descendants of Proust's characters. The inhabitants of this world liked to be invited to Embassy parties and were quite pleased to meet members of the Government there, though there were always *placement* problems as between Cabinet Ministers and Dukes; the Dukes, in the official setting of an Embassy, had to go further down the table but didn't like it. The 'monde' were quite welcoming and well disposed towards Iris and me. This was not entirely because of our personal charms. The Minister at the Paris Embassy has often come back later as Ambassador, and the Paris world, anxious to remain on the Embassy's invitation list, saw no harm in being polite to potential future occupants of the Hôtel de Charost. So we were invited to those alarming dinner-parties familiar to readers of *The Blessing* and *Don't Tell Alfred*. At these parties the food and the clothes were dazzling, and the conversation, almost always general, hardly less so. There was a tough quickness about it that posed great difficulties for slower-witted foreigners. I remember one dinner given on New Year's Eve by a Gaullist député, Max Brusset. As midnight struck the host went round kissing the ladies. On his right was a lady, of no great physical charms, who was reputed to be a great arranger of political appointments. Apparently satisfied by the chaste salute imprinted on her forehead she exclaimed, 'Vous serez Ministre!' But Henri Bernstein, sitting opposite, said in his bass rumble, 'En la baisant sur le front il a raté sa Présidence du Conseil.' It was not easy to compete with this kind of thing. But we more or less kept our ends up, and the 'Cocktail d'Adieu' which the Harveys gave for us when we left was attended by numerous Dukes, Princes and Marquises, besides most of the Cabinet.

Paris was also much frequented by royalty, exiled and otherwise. Princess Margaret came over for her first visit, to attend a ball in aid of the British Hospital which we organized, and the negotiations with Balmain for a ball-dress for Iris on this occasion were almost more prolonged and arduous than those about the European Defence Community in which I was concurrently involved. The Windsors dined with us, and I remember the Duke prefacing one remark with the comment, 'I happened to be King at the time.' The Kabaka, 'King Freddy', came to tea; many years later I attended his funeral in Kampala. On another occasion Iris's diary records that an unhappy Balkan ex-Queen 'came to see William. She has lost her baby and her husband.' Her situation, however, was less tragic than that of the Queen of Jordan who one day was shown into my office, in the Ambassador's temporary absence, and told me that her husband had gone out of his mind and was trying to kill her and her children. Her own Embassy could not protect her, and the Ambassador, who shortly afterwards returned, invited her and her younger children to stay. Later that day the King appeared in the Embassy courtyard and rushed round it banging on all the doors. Anxious faces watched from the windows, but he was unable to force his way in and eventually drove away. Soon after the Crown Prince, now King Hussein, then a schoolboy at Harrow, came over and took efficient charge of the situation, sending his mother and his brothers and sisters off to Switzerland and arranging for his father to go to hospital.

Not all our visitors were royal. Churchill spent some (for us) exhilarating days in Paris in January 1951. The Ambassador invited Paul Reynaud to meet him at dinner one night, and I heard Churchill say to Reynaud, 'Perhaps you remember that offer of common citizenship I made to France in 1940 when you were Prime Minister. What did you think of it? I was never sure it was a good idea.' On another evening Jules Moch brought along a copy of Churchill's speeches for Churchill to sign. Looking at it fondly Churchill said, 'Anyway we had much the best of the speeches in the last war, that fellow Hitler wasn't up to much in that respect.' Later that evening he said, 'I could have defended the British Empire against anyone (pause) against *anyone* (pause), except the British.' He was not a good listener; I spent some time trying to interpret to him a rather complicated tribute that Bidault, then Foreign Minister, was paying him, without much success, so that in the end poor Bidault put his head in his hands, crying, 'Il ne veut pas m'écouter, il ne veut pas m'écouter.'

Some of our other visitors, of whom there were all too many in those days, were less enjoyable. When Iris rang up the wife of a senior British official visiting Paris to ask her to dinner she said, so Iris's diary records, 'Before I had any time to say anything, that she had people waiting, then asked the name of a toyshop, then said, "What do you want?" and when told said her secretaries would let me know.' When she did consent to come she got her husband's secretary to ring up two hours before dinner to arrange a special menu for her. Another painful occasion was a speech by Harold Nicolson in May 1952 to a largely French audience, in which he said he had a permanent memorial to the fall of France because it had caused him to give up smoking and as a result he had put on two stone in weight.

Owing to the pressures of French social life, purely diplomatic entertainment tended to be squeezed out and played little part in our lives. But there was some of it. I lunched once with the Nuncio, Cardinal Roncalli, later Pope John XXIII, but can recall nothing of it except his two soft, pudgy hands clasping mine. I am afraid we all failed to detect the qualities of this very holy man, and our Heads of Mission report described him as 'a typical soapy Italian priest'. As doyen of the Diplomatic Corps he had to make a speech on behalf of us all at the annual diplomatic reception at the Elysée; his French was almost unintelligible, but hardly worse than that of the President of the Republic, Vincent-Auriol, who spoke with a thick Toulousian accent.

I was not in Paris all the time. We travelled a great deal. The Ambassador was always being invited to great wine celebrations. He would accept the major ones himself, to Burgundy or to Bordeaux, but would send me off to minor ones in delicious places like the Sarthe or Anjou, where we would stay with the préfet and be given wonderful dinners, with everything, the crayfish, the mushrooms, the fruit, from local woods and streams, and a succession of enchanting local wines which somehow never tasted quite so good when one got them back to Paris. We would also take at least one holiday a year in a different part of France; perhaps the most memorable was ten days one April staying at the Père Bise at Talloire, on the Lac d'Annecy, combining the most beautiful scenery in France with its most famous restaurant; by day we would walk up to the snow-line where the crocuses and snowdrops were just appearing as the snow melted, and at night we would eat *omble chevalier* and the other delicacies of that wonderful *cuisine*.

A more extended travel was one we made to French North Africa. The Air Attaché in those days had a private aeroplane, a Dove, which was nominally maintained to transport the Ambassador around. But Oliver Harvey had asthma and did not like flying. The Air Attaché was always afraid his aircaft might be withdrawn because under-used, and was keen for me to make use of it. The Maghreb was then still part of the French Empire, and the British Consulates there were under the jurisdiction of the British Embassy in Paris. It was arranged that I should visit them in the Air Attaché's plane in February 1952. We were still in a period of court mourning after the death of King George VI, and Iris had to travel in pitch-black clothes; the faces of the Consuls' wives who came to meet us in red hats were seen to drop as Iris appeared, black as a crow, at the aircraft's door. We visited Rabat, Casablanca, Marrakesh and Fez in Morocco, and also Algiers and Tunis. Apart from the odious Casablanca, which was like Shanghai all over again, noisy, provincial-cosmopolitan and corrupt, the Moroccan towns were splendid, particularly of course Marrakesh and Fez, so alike and so unlike, Marrakesh all a fierce dull red, the colour of dried blood, and Fez so elegantly white and green, the old towns so splendidly intact and alive and untouched by modern conveniences, with neat little French towns built alongside at a polite distance. Rabat was more surprising. From the way the French in Paris talked of the grandeur of the French Resident-General, I had expected viceregal splendours like those of New Delhi, and was quite startled by General Guillaume's over-grown villa. The French position in these territories, so soon to disappear, seemed stable enough then. Algeria, we were told, was and would always remain a Department of Metropolitan France. Tunis seemed calm enough under its puppet Bey, on whom I was taken to call, an absurd old gentleman with bright blue eyes and dyed red hair, wearing carpet slippers. It is true there was a slightly sinister feeling about Tunis's beautiful vaulted bazaars, but I felt quite jealous of the British Consul-General living in his charming Turkish palace out in the country near Carthage, a present to Queen Victoria from a former Bey, with its private railway station labelled 'Consulat Anglais', standing among fields full of blue, red and purple anemones.

But of course all this, these travels, this social activity, these royal and other visitors, were peripheral to my main job in Paris. This was dealing with the French Government and with Anglo-French relations. The Fourth Republic was a contradictory phenomenon. On the face of it it was absurd. Once de Gaulle had withdrawn from the scene its Governments changed every six months or so. The Communists were expelled from the Government, for good, a few months after the General's withdrawal, but their control of thirty per cent or so of the votes in Parliament, added to the twenty per cent or so of dissidents on the right, meant that there was never a stable majority. Arithmetically perhaps there could have been one, formed by the Socialists, the Catholic M.R.P., and the Radicals, but the opposition were always able to split up this natural coalition by introducing motions about religious education or similar topics which at once divided the coalition parties and brought the government down; a long and tedious process of cabinet-making then followed, with no one obviously in control. In all the international meetings of this period France had to be given a seat among the Great Powers because she owns, in fact she is, the most important piece of real estate in Europe, but she seemed hopelessly weak and lacking in prestige. Actually however the situation was nothing like as bad as it looked. The powerfully organized and able civil servants carried on the administration. Even the ministerial instability was less than it seemed; it merely reshuffled the pack, and in all this period, though there were many Prime Ministers, there were only two Foreign Ministers, Robert Schuman and Georges Bidault. Finally, the natural strength of France's economy was reasserting itself after the strains of the war, which were anyway less in France's case than in many others since she had done so little fighting. The economic recovery was handicapped by massive and determined tax evasion, but even this could not prevail against the economy's natural resilience, and in addition France had an unusual piece of good fortune; her recovery programme was under the direction of one of the few economic and political geniuses of the post-war period, Jean Monnet, whose Commissariat du Plan prepared an economic revival that matured just as the Fourth Republic fell, handing over a splendid going concern to de Gaulle's Fifth Republic which reaped undeserved credit for it.

But Monnet was not only concerned to re-plan France. He was busy re-planning Europe. A neat, dapper, determined little man, the inheritor of a splendid firm of Cognac distillers, his quiet, bourgeois exterior concealed a revolutionary spirit. 'The whole thing has got to be changed entirely' was a recurrent phrase in his conversation. The existing forms of government in Western Europe would not do. They had led to endless wars and must be replaced. But this must be done gradually. The right method was to introduce financial links, of a supranational character, which would so mix up the economies of the West European countries, particularly of France and Germany, that war between them would become a technical impossibility. Existing attempts at organizing the Western Powers, like the Office of European Economic Co-operation or N.A.T.O., were ineffective because they were merely alliances of sovereign nations and could be dissolved like other alliances. The supranational element was essential. For this reason Great Britain must not be allowed to join in the first instance. Monnet was extremely pro-British and had in fact been a British civil servant for the latter part of the war. But his reason for excluding us was perfectly logical. The French, then very much afraid of German domination, would have paid at that stage a high price for British participation, seen as an essential counterweight to Germany. Monnet was sure that, given our insular traditions, the price we should demand would be the elimination of the supranational elements in his scheme; this price would have been gladly paid by the French and his scheme would thus have been destroyed, so our entry at that stage must be prevented. But he was sure that once his supra-national communities were established the British would want to join and could then be admitted on the communities' own terms. All this came true in the end, though of course he failed to foresee the ludicrous de Gaulle interlude.

I knew all this because I was at this time seeing a good deal of Monnet. The Ambassador had delegated to me the task of contact with Monnet's plans, and I had frequent conversations with him. I found his argumentation on all this very convincing, so much so

4

that I was led into something of an indiscretion. Shortly after the announcement of what was then called the Schumann Plan; i.e. the proposal for a European Coal and Steel Community, Robert Schuman, its nominal author (it was in fact of course written by Monnet) who was then Foreign Minister, was invited to speak about it at a luncheon of the Anglo-American Press Club. I was also a guest at the luncheon, and when Schuman had finished speaking I got up and said that I believed most of the British people wished the Schuman Plan well, because they saw in it the germ of a real Franco-German reconciliation, which they believed to be a British interest. I said this because the Plan had been under severe and I thought unjustified attack in a certain section of the British press. But I was ticked off by the Foreign Office for having spoken out of turn. Matters became worse when I made another indiscreet speech on another topic a few weeks later. The president of the Anglo-American Press Club rang me up to say that a speaker had let them down and could I fill the gap? I made what seemed to me a few innocuous remarks about the necessity of establishing priorities of Government spending between defence and social services (this was just after the outbreak of the Korean War, which had induced a near-panic in Paris, many of my richer friends being engaged in rolling up their valuable pictures in preparation for a quick getaway before the Russians arrived, talking of emigrating, preferably to Corsica). My remarks seemed to me so innocuous that it never even occurred to me to say that they were off the record. But one of the journalists present, representing one of the more sensational London newspapers, chose to intepret them as a prior indication that the Attlee government intended to cut the social services, and his paper published an article to that effect. This led to rumours of a Parliamentary Question and to another ticking off for me from the Foreign Office.

However it did not lead apparently to any loss of confidence in me as the liaison with Monnet and his plans, and this became much more important and active with the launching of a new one, the so-called Pleven Plan for a European Defence Community (E.D.C.). This too was a product of Monnet's office, but a rather unwilling one. He would have preferred military integration to come at a later stage in his programme. But the Korean War had led to great pressure for German rearmament. Monnet feared that the creation of separate German armed forces would be a threat to his programme of integration as a whole, and it would indeed at that stage have been quite unacceptable to French opinion. So he produced his proposal for an integrated force of all the six Community States, which was called the Pleven Plan after the then Prime Minister. A committee of the six States was set up to work out the details, and to this British and American observers were attached. The American observer, David Bruce, was very active, both in and out of the interminable meetings, in pushing the plan forward. I as the British observer was more passive, but I was under constant pressure to secure a British contribution. Eventually the British Government were persuaded to give under-takings about a British share in Western European defence which were considered binding enough, and a treaty was drawn up and signed by the six States. It was never ratified, and its final collapse, which took place in 1954, after I left Paris, was a severe set-back to all Monnet's plans for European integration, which remained in the doldrums until they were successfully re-launched with the creation of the European Economic Community in 1957.

It is interesting to note that there was no serious expectation of, or pressure for, British participation in the E.D.C., and almost no advocates of it on the British side. One exception was Field-Marshal Montgomery. His views on this subject followed a somewhat erratic course. He was then in Paris as Deputy to General Eisenhower, at that time Supreme Commander of Allied Forces in Europe. I met the Field-Marshal, one evening in the early days of the E.D.C. negotiations, at dinner with the British Military Attaché. 'The E.D.C. is the greatest military nonsense ever invented,' he said, 'the greatest military nonsense ever invented.' (He always said everything twice.) I reminded him that his chief, General Eisenhower, was publicly committed to support of the E.D.C. 'Never mind that,' he said, 'I know about these things. You can take it from me that it's a military nonsense, a military nonsense.' A few months later he was telling everyone he met that Britain ought to join the E.D.C. I happened to meet him again at about this time, and reminded him of his previous description of it as a military nonsense, and also the fact that the policy of the British Government, whose servant he was, was opposed to British participation. He brushed this aside. 'I know the French,' he said (this was quite untrue; though he had been living in France for some time he knew virtually no French and had few French contacts). 'I know the French. They won't join unless Britain comes in.'

Though there was a certain apparent incompatibility between the Field-Marshal's two pronouncements they were, in fact, both true. The E.D.C., in the form propounded by Monnet, probably was a military nonsense; Monnet's knowledge of military matters was slight, and his plan of integrating national armies down to battalion level was almost certainly unworkable. It was equally true that one of the reasons for the final French refusal to ratify was dislike of a situation in which Great Britain would retain independent armed forces, while France would find hers fused into an integrated European army.

The lack of pressure in England at that time for British participation in any of the European communities perhaps needs some explanation, and my own experience is possibly typical. I later became (and remain) a strong supporter of British 'entry into Europe', and after my resignation from the Diplomatic Service wrote a series of articles in the *Observer* advocating this. But it never occurred to me, in the early fifties, that it was either possible or desirable. I remember drafting for the Ambassador an eloquent despatch about the fateful decision awaiting the French, the result of which might be the reduction of the historic assembly in the Palais Bourbon to the status of a county council. It never occurred to me that a similar fate might one day hang over that other even more historic assembly in the Palace of Westminster. I was still a victim of delusions about Great Britain's importance in the world; I thought the Commonwealth was a reality and the special relationship with America a permanence, and believed that all this put us on quite a different footing from the other nations of Western Europe. Moreover it seemed to me that there was another obstacle to British participation. All the six participating States had been defeated and occupied during the war, and most of them had recently improvised new national institutions to which they were not particularly attached and which could easily give way, I thought, to Monnet's new supranational institutions. Great Britain, on the other hand, had been neither defeated nor occupied, and she remained attached to her institutions which could not be included among the things which, in Monnet's recurrent phrase, would have to be 'changed entirely'. This too made her participation in Monnet's plans seem improbable to me, and I remained sceptical about his belief that we should eventually apply to be allowed in. I was convinced, however, that the success of his plans for the Six was a British interest, not only because it would strengthen the resistance of Western Europe to communist influences, which was then a real and pressing problem, but also because it seemed to point to the end of those Franco-German quarrels which had so often involved Great Britain in European wars. With the Ambassador's backing I impressed this view as strongly as I could upon the Foreign Office, and this may have had some effect in converting their original attitude of suspicious hostility towards Monnet's proposals into one of benevolent, though non-participating, support.

I gathered that the way all this had gone was generally approved in London and that my stock was high there. This was just as well because I could see that my days in Paris were numbered. The Ambassador was due to retire in 1954, and it was clearly desirable that my successor should be well installed and run in before the change occurred. We had already begun preparing for the change by taking Teresa away from her Paris school and putting her into a boarding school in England, to the horror of our French servants; 'Pauvre Mademoiselle,' said Julie, our cook, 'qu'est-ce qu'elle a fait?' (French children are not normally sent to a boarding school unless they are delinquent.) But of course the main question was, where were we going?

At the end of March 1953 Iris and I were on holiday in Provence. We were driving about without any particular plan, and the only address we had left was Poste Restante at Arles. On March 20th we passed through Arles for the last time, after a long and tiring day in the Camargue, on our way to Les Baux. Rather casually we looked into the post office for mail, and found a telegram from the Ambassador in Paris telling me to get in touch immediately with the Consul-General at Marseille 'who has an important communication for you'. I rang up Marseille. A Vice-Consul answered the telephone, and I asked for the message.

'I'm sorry,' he said, 'I'm not allowed to telephone it.'

'Then put it in the post to Les Baux.'

'I'm sorry, I'm not allowed to post it.'

'I'm not coming down to Marseille to collect it,' I said. 'It's hot and we're tired.'

'Well, what do you suggest?' asked the Vice-Consul. This was a false move. As Minister at the Embassy I was in a sense his superior officer.

'I suggest you should drive up here with it,' I replied. This was a suggestion I should not have dared to make if he had not given me such an opening.

There was a sigh at the other end of the telephone. 'I'll be with you in two hours.'

'Before you start,' I said, 'can you tell me one thing? Does it concern my next post?'

'It does.'

While we waited for him, Iris and I walked round the Arles boulevards, speculating. For some time past we had been making various guesses about our future. Vienna was where we wanted to go. It seemed to be about our level, and I liked the idea of returning there. We had even let our hopes be known in what we thought was the right quarter. But it seemed too good to be true. We wondered about other places. Iris mentioned Moscow. 'Much too senior for me,' I said. Eventually we gave up, took a room at a hotel and waited in silence for the Vice-Consul. When he arrived we were tremendously British and restrained, ordered drinks and settled him down. 'Now,' I said, 'what is this mysterious communication?'

It turned out to be an inquiry whether I would go to Moscow as Ambassador. The happy dreams of Vienna faded, but obviously the prospect was too interesting for any hesitation. The promotion was, too, a dazzling one. At the age of forty-six I not only now became the youngest British Ambassador serving anywhere, I was also to hold one of the most important Embassies, and at a particularly interesting juncture too (Stalin had just died, and the situation in the Soviet Union was evolving critically). My career had passed the stage of being promising; it could now be said to be definitely successful.

However there then followed a twilit period while my appointment was still secret. The news broke on April 12th, after our return to Paris, and created a mild sensation. The moment was, as I have said, an interesting one, and my own appointment was in itself an innovation; most previous British Ambassadors had been sent there at the end of their careers, after having previously been the heads of several missions elsewhere, whereas this was to be my first (and as it turned out my last) post as head of a mission. So there was a good deal of telephoning and a number of articles in the Press, some of them critical. We left Paris on June 12th, and after an interval in London during which I kissed hands and was knighted, and made rather unsuccessful attempts to brush up my rusty and inadequate Russian, we left for Moscow on October 1st in a R.A.F. transport plane.

SIX

A Difficult Embassy

i. First Impressions

As we flew into Moscow we could see white pointed towers gleaming in the sun against an inky sky. For a moment I got the scale wrong and thought that they were the towers of the Kremlin painted white again, as they used to be in the eighteenth century; then I saw that they were the new Stalin skyscrapers that had been built up in a ring round the old city since I had last been there in 1945, gargantuan replicas, in silhouette at least, of the Kremlin towers.

It is customary for an ambassador newly arrived at his post to send a despatch to the Foreign Office recording his first impressions. I conformed to this custom, but with some reluctance. Of what value, I asked, were the reactions of a gold-fish in a bowl, peering through opaque and refracting glass at an utterly alien world, all contact with which was denied him? Besides, I added, my reactions lacked even the virtue of freshness; I had been in this particular bowl before. But in fact Moscow seemed to have changed very little since 1945, except for those white skyscrapers I had seen gleaming as we flew in. These were the great monuments of the post-war Stalin era. As such they were already beginning to be unpopular, and one of them, the Hotel Ukraine, seemed to be almost literally hanging its head in shame; its topmost pinnacle was definitely out of the perpendicular. When Mr. Duncan Sandys, then Minister of Housing, came to visit Moscow in May 1956 I took him to visit Khrushchev. Mr. Sandys had taken a great fancy to these skyscrapers, and I warned him not to praise them to Khrushchev. He ignored this warning, and was rewarded by a tirade against their wasteful extravagance. Apart from the skyscrapers Moscow remained unreconstructed.

I commented in my initial despatch that there were, within a few hundred yards of the Embassy, slums that reminded me more of wartime Chungking than of any European capital with which I was familiar. Stalin had neglected housing in favour of prestige projects, a neglect which lay heavily on his successors and which they began gradually to repair.

But though Moscow was superficially unaltered there were already signs of significant changes in other respects. An interesting one occurred at the very moment of my arrival. Until then the British and American Ambassadors, wherever they went, were always followed closely by two guards from the secret police (this attention was confined to these two Ambassadors, and a previous French Ambassador is said to have protested officially to the Soviet Ministry of Foreign Affairs that his exclusion from this privilege was a slight to France's status as a Great Power). Joe Gascoigne, my predecessor, on his final departure had been accompanied to the airport by his two faithful followers, and when I arrived the Embassy staff who had come to meet us looked round for them. But they never appeared, and when the American Ambassador returned from leave a few days later he found that his guard too had been withdrawn.

This was one of many pointers towards a general relaxation of secret police control. Beria had been arrested in the previous July (his execution was to be announced the following December),* and it soon became apparent that in this respect at least there was to be a marked contrast with my previous Moscow period. Then our contacts with Russians had been limited to a few dozens, the officials with whom we dealt, our Russian teachers, our servants. Even among these few there were constant arrests and unexplained disappearances. In my time as Ambassador from 1953 onwards we got to know hundreds, perhaps thousands of Soviet

---

* Beria's disappearance had various rather macabre consequences. His house, which became an Embassy, was said to be haunted and had to be exorcized. And the British Embassy, which like most others was a subscriber to the *Great Soviet Encyclopaedia*, received a circular communication from the editors suggesting that certain pages be cut out (we were recommended to use a sharp razor) and replaced by a long, boring article on the Bering Sea. The excised pages contained a laudatory article about Beria.

citizens, none of them well but all of them enough to know what became of them, and among all this great number we never heard of any single case of a political arrest. However one may criticize Stalin's successors in other respects, they deserve enormous credit for this undoubted alleviation of the permanent, if fluctuating, reign of terror under Stalin.

My own reception followed the lines normal elsewhere. I presented my letters of credence in the Kremlin within a few days of my arrival. As we were walking in the *chef de protocole* said to me, 'Do you pronounce it Walter or Valter?'

'It's Walter,' I said, 'but why do you ask?'

'I have to announce your name, Sir Walter Hayter.'

'It's Sir William, not Sir Walter.'

'Oh yes of course, tut, tut, how silly of me.'

The doors were then flung open, and he announced in stentorian tones, 'Sir Walter Hayter.'

I also paid the usual calls on the officials of the Ministry of Foreign Affairs. Not one of these was familiar to me from the thirties. Then the People's Commissariat for Foreign Affairs, as it was called, was staffed almost entirely by Jews of the Litvinov type, cultivated and internationally inclined. These had all disappeared in the Purges and had been replaced by a new generation formed in Molotov's image. The most notable of these was Gromyko, whom I had known as Soviet Counsellor in Washington when I was First Secretary there, and again at the Potsdam Conference when we sat on the same sub-committee and he had astonished and rather disconcerted me by the skill and rapidity with which he drafted complicated diplomatic documents in English.

At my first interview with Molotov, then Minister of Foreign Affairs, I made the request, routine elsewhere, to call on the Prime Minister, then Malenkov. Such requests, though frequently made by Ambassadors in Stalin's time, were usually ignored in Moscow, and my predecessor had only had one short interview with Stalin during his whole time as Ambassador. However a few weeks later Gromyko informed me, when I was calling on him on another matter, that Malenkov would see me next day at eleven. He added with a wintry smile that this meant eleven a.m., an allusion to the fact that when Stalin did condescend to receive anyone it was usually in the middle of the night; the more normal hour was clearly an indication of more normal methods of working. Nothing of any interest passed at that meeting, but I was able to report to the Foreign Office that the new Prime Minister, whose personality was then quite unknown, did not seem to be of the overbearing, daemonic dictator type but more of a business-like and clear-headed politician.

As I was the first Ambassador whom Malenkov had received since he became Prime Minister some nine months before, my interview with him created a mild sensation. But it was in fact only one sign of the policy of increased accessibility which the new Soviet leaders were adopting. There had been a notable demonstration of this a few weeks earlier during the usual anniversary celebrations of the October Revolution, which for reasons not worth explaining falls on November 7th. At the Soviet Government's reception that evening Iris and I had been invited to Molotov's table and found ourselves, with other Ambassadors and distinguished foreigners, seated among the whole Party leadership, with the notable exceptions of Malenkov and Khrushchev. It was the first Soviet essay in this mode, and not a wholly successful one; the American Ambassador, for instance, found himself next to the East German leader Ulbricht with whom, once identified, no conversation was permissible. But every attempt was made to make the occasion a jolly one, with speeches and toasts, Molotov as usual showing himself an excellent host. This was the first of many occasions on which foreign Ambassadors were privileged to observe Bulganin, then Minister of Defence, in a state of intoxication; on this occasion he got so drunk that he had to be led away and was replaced at the table by Marshal Zhukov, the great wartime hero; this was Zhukov's first appearance since his severe eclipse in Stalin's later years. The Ambassadors who had not been invited to the top table crowded round, so did numerous journalists and other guests, and I recorded afterwards that it felt like being the King of France dining in public.

Later on the Soviet leaders took to attending national day receptions and other similar functions in fair numbers and regularly. In Stalin's time only one or two minor officials would turn up at these parties, and the change was very notable. Of my own contacts with them, two early occasions remain most clearly in my memory. One was the dinner they gave to Chou En-lai, the Chinese Prime Minister, when he passed through Moscow in July 1954 on his way back from the Geneva Conference. Until that time no one had seen the Soviet and Chinese Communist leaders together, and there was much speculation about their relationship, the general assumption being that the Chinese were Soviet satellites. One sight of Chou En-lai in Khrushchev's company was enough to dispel that illusion. They were then still believed to be indissoluble allies, but it was notable to all of us who attended that quite small dinner that relations were not easy. Chou teased the Russians; he teased them about the non-appearance of their wives in public; he teased them about their refusal to learn any foreign languages; he teased them most of all by making a speech in English—'Excuse my poor English,' he said, and then spoke in excellent, fluent English, not one word of which was comprehensible to his Russian hearers. There were other speeches and toasts in which a lot was made of the populations each speaker represented; Chou claimed his six hundred millions, the Indian Ambassador his four hundred millions, I advanced my few poor fifty millions, and Khrushchev, in his turn, said he spoke for two hundred millions only but—turning to Chou—'we'll catch you up.' It was a joke, but there were barbed undertones. Chou came up after dinner as I was expounding to one of the Soviet leaders my current views on American policy; the Americans, I said, often said foolish things but very rarely did foolish things (this was in pre-Vietnam days). 'I hope you're right,' said Chou, 'I hope you're right.' A man of enormous, weary charm and obvious intelligence, it is easy to understand his seductive effect on Asian leaders.

The other occasion when I had an early opportunity of contacts with the Soviet leaders was in August of that same year, 1954, when a Labour Party delegation passed through Moscow on its way to China. The delegation was headed by Mr. Attlee (who stayed with us in the Embassy) and its other members included Aneurin Bevan, Morgan Phillips, Sam Watson and Dr. Edith Summerskill. It is customary in Embassies, if you have distinguished visitors from your own country, to invite their opposite numbers to meet them. The opposite number in Moscow of the Leader of the Opposition, as Mr. Attlee then was, was not easily identifiable. I thought of Khrushchev, not so much because there were then already signs of his opposition to Malenkov as because this was a party delegation and Khrushchev, who then had no official position, was the leading Secretary of the Communist Party. Accordingly I telephoned to Vyshinsky, then Vice-Minister of Foreign Affairs, and asked him if he would invite Khrushchev on my behalf. Next day Vyshinsky replied, very much to my surprise, that not only would Khrushchev come but that Malenkov, Mikoyan, Molotov, Vyshinsky himself, Shvernik (then Head of State), the Mayor of Moscow and various others, none of whom I had invited, would come too. Moreover we were all to dine with them the day before.

Though gratifying, this mass acceptance rather took my breath away. This was before the Presidium, as the Soviet leaders were then collectively known, had taken to going to parties. They had never dined in an Embassy before, and their personalities were very little known to the outside world. In Stalin's time they had been distantly visible, squat, flat-capped figures, on Lenin's tomb during ceremonial parades, and at wartime banquets they had been glimpsed rather more closely, muttering to each other and obediently drinking toasts when the Leader proposed them. But they could hardly be distinguished except by the presence or absence of moustaches or spectacles; they were all approximately the same size and shape, short, powerful men whom no one could really tell apart.

Obviously this was all much more interesting then than it is now, when we know so much about them all. Then it seemed very exciting, and when I returned to England on leave shortly afterwards I was specially invited down to Chartwell to tell the Prime Minister all about it (this was, I think, the third or fourth time that Sir Winston said to me, 'I have sent for you in order to make your acquaintance'—a greeting which was flattering and agreeable the first time it was used but less so on subsequent occasions). At the dinner with the Presidium, which took place in an attractive classical villa at Uspenskoye, about twenty-five miles from Moscow, the relationships of the Soviet leaders were interesting to watch. Malenkov was mostly silent, smiling and playing with a flower. Mikoyan was the court jester. Molotov was the genial, fatherly host. Khrushchev did most of the talking. No one had seen him in this way before, and the first impression was alarming. He seemed impulsive and blundering, and startlingly ignorant of foreign affairs. Bevan tried to put some quite simple United Nations point to him and he totally failed to grasp it, in spite of expert interpreting, until it was explained to him in words of one syllable by Malenkov. I reported afterwards that he seemed to me practical and cunning rather than intelligent, like a little bull who if aimed the right way would charge along and be certain to arrive with a crash at his objective, knocking down anything that was in his way. But it would require someone to aim him the right way, and it would be difficult to stop him once you had started him off. I added that he was not at all receptive to new ideas. This was a superficial judgment, as time was to show.

The dinner at the Embassy the next day was on similar lines. Stalin had once dined at the Embassy during the war, and then the whole building was taken over by the secret police. There were no special precautions this time. It all looked very fine, the big dining-room with its painted ceiling and red silk walls on which hung huge royal portraits (it was always necessary to explain to Russian guests that the portrait of George V was of him and not of the last Tsar Nicholas II, his first cousin whom he so closely resembled), the table loaded with the silver plate from 'Her Majesty's Embassy to the Porte' and rows of glasses. During dinner there were the usual toasts and speeches. Afterwards Bevan sat on a sofa with Malenkov, waving away the Embassy staff. No one wanted to be bothered with Khrushchev except Sam Watson, who did not get very far in his attempts to persuade the Soviet Party Secretary of the fallacies of Communism. I asked Mr. Attlee which of the Russians he would like to talk to; he was tired, said 'none of them', and sat down in a corner with Morgan Phillips. However Mikoyan insisted on joining them, and Mr. Attlee in annoyance attacked him violently about Marxism, astonishing Mikoyan by what seemed to him the perversity of his views. It was during this visit that I myself had a slightly alarming

conversation with Mr. Attlee. He suddenly said to me at breakfast: 'Have you read Marx?' This struck me as rather a loaded
question, coming from the head of the British Socialist Party to
the British Ambassador in a Marxist country. I said nervously that
I hadn't read it all but that I'd read the potted version supplied to
us by the Foreign Office. 'Haven't read any of it myself,' said
Mr. Attlee.

These were only the first of many occasions I was to have
during my time in Moscow to get to know the Soviet leaders.
Ultimately, as I recorded in my farewell despatch, I was able by a
series of lucky chances to see more of Russia's rulers than perhaps
any British Ambassador since Lord Malmesbury became the con-
fidant of Catherine the Great. This, I added, was a mixed blessing;
anyone associating with the great in Russia needed a strong
stomach, metaphorically even more than literally. Moreover these
contacts were not always very rewarding. Like my colleagues,
I had high hopes, when the Soviet leaders started their new policy
of accessibility, that this would mean the beginning of normal
diplomatic activity in Moscow. We would, we thought, engage
in frank, confidential discussion with our new friends, in which
the serious issues between the Soviet Union and the rest of the
world would be sorted out in genuine dialogues. But it did not
turn out like that. Each of the Soviet leaders carried his own
private Iron Curtain around with him. Responses were pre-
dictable; conversations were like *Pravda* leading articles on one
side and *The Times* leading articles on the other; well-grooved
long-playing records went round and round.

After a year in Moscow I discussed, in a despatch to the
Foreign Office, the quite genuine question whether it was worth
maintaining an Embassy in Moscow at all. I concluded, predict-
ably perhaps, that it was, in spite of its cost, then absurdly and
artificially high owing to the bogus rate of exchange maintained
by the Soviet Government. I thought there were three reasons
why an Embassy was useful. First, experience of the Soviet Union
was essential for members of the Diplomatic Service, all of whose
future work would be in one way or another conditioned by the
Soviet impact. Second, members of the Embassy could get, by
travel and otherwise, information about Soviet conditions not

otherwise available, and could sense the atmosphere. Third, though the Soviet leaders were clearly not yet prepared for serious negotiations, the presence of Western Embassies showed that we at least were ready and available if they were ever to want to talk.

This did not mean, however, that conditions for the practice of diplomacy in Moscow were any easier than in the past. In August 1590 Queen Elizabeth I sent a letter of complaint to Tsar Theodore, Ivan the Terrible's feeble son and successor. 'The entertainment that our Highness's Ambassadors and messengers receive of Your Majesty,' she wrote, 'is not agreeable to our princely quality, and not such as we show unto your Ambassadors and messengers, of what quality soever they be of, which we refer to their own reports. Yea, we are credibly informed that Your Majesty maketh more estimation of other princes of meaner quality; heathens, Tartars, Turks etc. receive better exceptance than ours in all respects.'

It is all there, the English Ambassador in Moscow with a grievance, the kindness to the Russians in London, the preference shown to Asian Ambassadors in Moscow; all is familiar.

'These gross injuries,' the Queen goes on, slightly losing control of her syntax in her indignation, 'whether it were tolerable by you if we should show the least of them towards Your Majesty; and the like were never offered of no prince towards us, no not of our greatest enemies, and altho' they are hardly to be digested of any princely nature, yet have we not been desirous of revenge or breach of brotherly relations.'

Familiar again, the hint of retaliation, which the Queen clearly knows perfectly well she cannot make effective. This is the true Moscow form. Diplomats are spies and must be cut off, isolated, if possible humiliated, except perhaps for a few favoured clients from Asia. The St. Petersburg period, when the Russian Government tried to ape European ways in their treatment of diplomats as in other respects, was the exception; when the Government returned to Moscow it reverted to type. In Stalin's time the isolation was at its most complete. There was, as I have recounted, a considerable relaxation after his death. His successors made a genuine attempt to establish social contacts with the outside

world. They entertained and they accepted hospitality. Not surprisingly, perhaps, they used this hospitality as a political instrument. They marked their pleasure or displeasure, for instance, by
the quantity and quality of their representation at an Embassy's
National Day reception. Iris's diary recalls that our first Queen's
Birthday Party, in 1954, was attended only by one member of
the Presidium, Mikoyan. Next year, in 1955, three came (Bulganin, Mikoyan, Pervukhin). In 1956, in the full flush of the
euphoria engendered by Bulganin's and Khrushchev's visit to
London, we had five (Bulganin, Khrushchev, Malenkov, Molotov, Zhukov). They also began to accept invitations to smaller
luncheons or dinners; Mikoyan, Malenkov, Furtseva and Kosygin
came in this way in my time. It was possible, too, to induce large
numbers of lesser Russians to accept the Embassy's hospitality to
meet their opposite numbers in some visiting delegation. There
were Parliamentary delegations, business men, trade unionists,
artists, sportsmen; all of these were lavishly entertained by the
Russians, and were generally glad that they could vicariously
return this hospitality when the Embassy invited them and their
hosts. In this way a really very large number of Russians of all
sorts and kinds passed through our gates. But the results were,
somehow, unreal. We never got to know any of them really well,
never could make the kind of genuine and lasting friendships we
had achieved in all our previous diplomatic posts, and were never
once invited inside a Russian home.

Not that the Russians were themselves inhospitable. They
gave immense and lavish official parties of all kinds. I have described some of them earlier in this chapter. Another, which was
significant for its curious political overtones, was given in June
1956 to the delegates who had been attending the Tushino air-
show. It was held in the open air, in a park, and after some curious
antics in the course of which the Secretary of State for Air, Mr.
Nigel Birch, was rowed about by Bulganin in a small dinghy on
an ornamental lake we all, the Presidium and a number of Ambassadors as well as the delegations, settled down to some heavy
drinking round a table in the open. Bulganin went hard at it, and
it was also the only occasion on which I myself ever saw Khrushchev the worse for drink. As Bulganin drank more and more he

became more and more sentimental. Khrushchev on the other hand became aggressive, and in a series of short speeches managed to insult literally every country in the world. First he said that only Great Powers counted, which put all the small countries in their place. Then he said only the United States and the Soviet Union mattered. France was too poor to make an atom bomb. The Royal Air Force (he was just back from his visit to England) had only obsolete bombers; I thought some of the numerous Air Marshals present were going to get apoplexy. Then he had his usual go at America and proposed a toast to China which the American Ambassador could not drink, and to East Germany which none of us could. There were no Chinese present at first but Molotov produced a little general from somewhere; Khrushchev ignored him. Bulganin stood up during some of Khrushchev's speeches and tried in a maudlin way to soften his asperities; Khrushchev told him to sit down. Molotov, Malenkov and Kaganovich at the other end of the table were pursing their lips and drumming their fingers on the arms of their chairs, and Kaganovich said to Molotov across a Western ambassadress: 'All this is very unnecessary.' Eventually Malenkov, Kaganovich and others brought the proceedings to a stop by remaining standing after one of Khrushchev's toasts and going round saying good-night. It was a kind of minor Anti-Party Plot in advance. All of this took place before a large audience of Russians and foreigners, including numerous journalists.

Most of our Russian parties were less dramatic than this. They were always lavish, they usually went on too long but they were well intended and it was rare that any attempt was made to force unwilling foreigners to drink more than was good for them. But they did not really contribute anything to international exchanges; the atmosphere was seldom conducive to serious talk, and the *bonhomie* so laboriously engendered always seemed a little synthetic.

The social duties of a British Embassy normally have a clearly defined order of priorities. The local inhabitants come first, then the diplomatic colleagues, then the British colony, then the Embassy staff. This order could not be strictly observed in Moscow. Local hospitality was subject to the limitations I have de-

scribed. There was virtually no resident British colony, apart
from one or two journalists. On the other hand entertaining the
Embassy staff had to be taken very seriously indeed and given a
high priority. The staff, especially the junior staff, inevitably lived
uncomfortable and generally confined and dull lives, and they
were at all times exposed to Soviet attempts at penetration. It was
essential to do everything possible to alleviate their dreary lot and
to give them a sense of community, and Iris's diary records almost
daily entertainments for them. One entry notes that on February
8th, 1954, among others 'a new Mr. Vassall' lunched with us. He
appears again as accompanying us to Leningrad in October of
1955, and the following month he came to a dinner-party of
thirty in honour of a naval attaché who was leaving. He is noted
as having been very amusing in a small part in an Embassy's production of Rattigan's *Harlequinade* in January 1956. By that time,
of course, he had been for some years in the employment of the
Soviet intelligence service. I remember him dimly as an obliging
little figure who was useful at tea parties. There was no excuse
for him. If he had come to me or to the Naval Attaché and told
us that he was being blackmailed by the Russians he could have
been sent home at once without any opposition from the Soviet
authorities. One or two similar cases occurred during my time,
and in none of them was there any difficulty about exit visas.
Vassall's timidity or folly amounted to a crime, and though I have
always doubted whether he was really a useful source of intelligence to the Russians he certainly caused a great many people a
great deal of trouble in the end.

This persecution of the Embassies by the Soviet intelligence
services was one of the least attractive features of Moscow life.
We were obliged to act on the assumption that all our rooms were
microphoned. Our servants were all believed to be spies (this had
its compensations. Spies are more intelligent, I suppose, than the
average domestic servant, and they cannot give you notice. Our
Russian servants were certainly all charming and very efficient.)
Things were less bad than in Stalin's time, but this uncomfortable
side of things had not been completely eliminated.

In all this, of course, we only shared the common lot of all our
diplomatic colleagues. In writing about Moscow in the thirties

I may have sounded a little condescending about the Moscow diplomatic corps of those days. Its calibre had enormously improved by the fifties, no doubt because of Moscow's enhanced importance on the international scene, and in fact the corps this time contained many remarkable men, some of them now in high positions in their own countries. Chip Bohlem, who was United States Ambassador during my whole time in Moscow and who later became Ambassador in Paris, and Louis Joxe who was French Ambassador and was subsequently a leading member of General de Gaulle's Government, were both old friends; we met frequently in each other's houses, and certainly while we were there Three-Power co-operation, which was then something active and real, never suffered from any conflicting views or any failure to communicate or co-ordinate between the three Embassies in Moscow.

This was the period of visits. The dark night of Stalinism was over, and distinguished foreigners poured in, Nehru, Adenauer and Tito, the Shah, Hammarskjöld and Soekarno, Harold Wilson and the Archbishop of York. Conspicuous absentees were the leaders of the three major Western Powers, though Guy Mollet, then Prime Minister of France, paid a brief visit in May 1956. Some of the visitors came to negotiate, some came to see. All were lavishly entertained. Great banquets, with the atmosphere of a court, were given in the Kremlin; the Ambassadors would line up in the St. Andrew's Hall, the door of the inner apartments would open, and out would come the Crown Prince of the Yemen, or the Prime Minister of Poland, or Prince Sihanouk of Cambodia, with the Presidium behind them, bowing and smiling. We would then move to the St. George's Hall, and there would be a concert; Oistrakh or Richter would play, Plissetskaya would dance the *Dying Swan*, Reisen would sing Prince Gremin's aria from *Eugène Onegin*. There would be toasts to the visitor, and to peace. The delegations, the Presidium, the Ambassadors would stand grouped round little tables, drinking vodka or Armenian brandy and eating caviar and smoked sturgeon. The white marble walls, covered with the gilded names of the holders of the Tsarist Order of St. George, reflected the glitter of immense chandeliers.

These parties were an entertainment in themselves. But they

were not the only form of entertainment available in Moscow. The theatre had deteriorated since the thirties. The Moscow Arts Theatre had ossified; the same classics were being played in the same productions, sometimes even with the same actors in the same parts they were taking in 1937; Tarasova, for instance, was Anna Karenina in 1937 and Anna Karenina in 1957. Most of the other theatres were merely inferior imitations of the Moscow Arts; the experimental producers like Meyerhold and Tairov had disappeared in the Purges. Almost the only life in the theatre, then, was oddly enough in the Puppet Theatre. Obrastsov, its director, became almost a friend; he visited England twice during this period and wrote the first sympathetic account of it in a little book he published on his return. Some of his puppets gave charming performances at two of the annual Christmas parties we used to give to the children of the diplomatic corps. The Bolshoi continued on its ponderous, magnificent way. Productions of Russian opera were still splendid, but of course one went there mainly to see ballet. It was easy to criticize the Bolshoi Ballet in those days; its repertoire was limited (*Swan Lake* and *Sleeping Beauty*, *Romeo and Juliet* and *Cinderella*, *The Fountain of Bakhchiserai* and occasional performances of *Giselle*, *Don Quixote* and one or two others, all full-length ballets), the décors were Edwardian, and as far as choreography and production were concerned Diaghilev, Fokin and Massine might never have been born. It was splendid, nevertheless. It had two superlative and quite dissimilar ballerinas in Ulanova and Plissetskaya; the men were solid, the *corps de ballet* perfect, and a kind of magic was generated by almost every performance. *Swan Lake* was performed at practically every one of the galas given to the numerous State visitors in those days, and we must have seen it at least twenty times; it never palled. Visiting the Ballet School was another enormous pleasure; it was touching to see the little creatures with their skinny arms sketching out the grand gestures so familiar to us from the Bolshoi stage, and the charming directress, Madame Bocharnikova, was very kind to us.

Achieving fresh air and exercise, never a fetish of mine but strongly advocated by Iris, was not easy in Moscow. The British Embassy then possessed the only tennis-court in the capital, or at any rate the only one visible to foreigners, and this could be flooded and used for skating in the winter. However as I neither play tennis nor skate this was no solution as far as I was concerned. The solution was in fact to go for long walks in the country, on skis in the winter. Moscow, though so large, ends abruptly, and splendidly unspoiled country reaches up to its walls. We came to be deeply attached to this Moscow countryside, nightingales singing in every bush, the woods full of lilies of the valley in spring and of purple and yellow salvias in the summer, the pale golden birches in the autumn and the heavy covering of snow in the winter.

One winter expedition had an odd sequel. We had been for a long walk on skis near Archangelskoye, where the Yusopovs used to live. We went too far, got rather lost and were very late returning to the Embassy. It was perhaps just as well because when we did get back we were met in the courtyard by an agitated member of the staff who said, 'You can't go upstairs, there's a bandit in the dining-room.' It seemed that a man with a revolver had shot (not fatally) a militiaman on duty outside the gate and had rushed past the security guard in the hall and up the stairs to our part of the house. The guard and one of the diplomatic secretaries, believing that we were already upstairs and in need of protection, had gallantly hurried up, unarmed, after him. As they approached him he said, brandishing his revolver, 'Are you English or Russian?' It was not quite clear to them which the right answer was, so they closed on him in silence. He allowed himself to be disarmed and asked for asylum in the Embassy.

It was at this point that we got back, and the matter was referred to me for decision. It was quite clear to me that we could not give political asylum to a man who had shot a policeman, and I ordered that he should be handed over. While we were waiting for the Soviet authorities to collect him members of my staff had some talk with him; he was clearly deranged.

This somewhat dramatic incident was not typical of our Moscow life. It came to a disturbed close, but on the whole it was peaceful, busy, interesting and surprisingly luxurious. The British Embassy is a fine if slightly absurd house. It was built in the late nineteenth century by a sugar millionaire who wanted a little bit of everything, so that although the exterior is a fairly uniform example of nineteenth-century Italianate the interior is a kind of fruit-salad. An immense Gothic staircase, lined with false Gobelins, leads to a 'Louis Quinze' dining-room, beyond which is an 'Empire' ballroom, a 'Renaissance' smoking-room and so on. This is all right when the doors are closed, but when they are open and the Gothic fumed oak projects into the red silk of the 'Louis Quinze' the effect is bizarre. However it was very comfortable to live in and the view, of the Kremlin across the river, must be the best from any British Embassy in the world.

I have always maintained that to enjoy diplomatic life in Moscow you must be one of two things, a bachelor secretary with no ties or responsibilities, able to travel and get about, or an Ambassador luxuriously installed in an Embassy with plenty of people to look after you. I was lucky enough to have both of these, and could easily see that diplomats whose career brought them there in the intervening phase, newly married and with young children, would find it all much less enjoyable than I did.

ii. Soviet Personalities

In the last section I mentioned three reasons why it seemed to me worth while to maintain an Embassy in Moscow. I might have added a fourth, the opportunity that we in Moscow had to study Soviet personalities. After all, most of the information available to us in the Embassy was equally available to any good press-cutting agency in London with a knowledge of Russian. But in Moscow we had one unique advantage, the ability to observe at close range those strange, powerful figures the Soviet leaders, on whose whims, temperaments and convictions so much of the future of the world depended. This was a topic to which we all devoted a great deal of attention and many reports, and it may be of some interest to record my impressions of the leading figures of my Moscow period.

Undoubtedly the two most important were Malenkov and Khrushchev, at that time the contenders for supremacy. Malenkov was Stalin's nominated heir, and at first succeeded to control of

both the Party and the Government, though he soon ceded the
Party to Khrushchev. He was (it is difficult not to talk of him in
the past tense, though so far as anyone knows he is still alive) a
small dark man with sleek hair and a smooth, sallow skin. There
was something creepy about his appearance, like a eunuch,
though he could produce a charming smile. He was quick, clever
and subtle, not in a hurry; when the American Ambassador and
I had a long talk with him at the Kremlin banquet in November
1954 he kept repeating, '*Terpeniye, terpeniye i terpeniye*' ('patience,
patience and patience'), and we both thought this was perhaps the
key to his character. He had been Stalin's most faithful henchman
in his later days and must have had many terrible things on his
conscience; but as we got to know him in 1953 and 1954 we all
concluded that though tough and secretive he was a man with
whom business could be done. We were sure he would be more
than a match for the apparently clumsy and impetuous Khrushchev, and it was a surprise as well as a disappointment to most of
us in Moscow when he resigned in February 1955. Probably his
weakness was that in Stalin's time he had been too much in the
great man's shadow, too much of a back-room boy, to build up
sufficient personal following within the Party apparatus, so that
when Khrushchev got the apparatus under his control Malenkov
was left friendless.

Khrushchev was very different. I have recorded my first, misleading impressions of him in the last section. He seemed to me
rumbustious, impetuous, loquacious, free-wheeling, alarmingly
ignorant of foreign affairs. But a little reflexion should have
shown us that this first impression was necessarily wrong. Ignorant of foreign affairs he certainly was, but this was not surprising;
he had until then been solely concerned with internal questions,
and as soon as he applied his powerful intelligence and his en-
cyclopaedic memory to foreign affairs he mastered them completely. He was loquacious, true, but his loquacity was under
control; it had to be, or he could never have survived in such close
proximity to the pathologically suspicious Stalin, ferociously
watching for the slightest indiscretion. And indeed if one listened
to his loquacity one observed that, though vivid and folksy in its
expression, its content stuck to the strictest Party orthodoxy.

When Khrushchev began to come to the fore it became necessary to try to make him real to people in London. This was not at first easy. London was used to having only to bother about one leader in Russia. This, they decided, was now Malenkov. He was the Prime Minister and the official heir, and they thought they could pronounce his name (though they always pronounced it wrong, putting the accent on the second instead of on the last syllable). Khrushchev was somehow invisible; he had no identifiable position and his name was obviously unpronounceable. To get round this difficulty, to try to make London see him, I used to use two analogies.

The first was with the typical Russian peasant as he appears in the classical Russian novels of the nineteenth century, sly, shrewd, suspicious, cautious under an appearance of abandon, fundamentally contemptuous of the *barin*, the master. Their classic literary appearance is in the famous scene in *Anna Karenina* where Levin goes to mow the hay with his peasants. Levin, the *barin*, is big, strong and well-fed and they are small and undernourished; but they mow much more hay than he does and despise him for his amateur efforts. Khrushchev, I said, was like one of those peasants raised to the nth power.

The other, less literary comparison was with a British trades union leader of the old-fashioned kind, Arthur Deakin or Ernest Bevin. The analogies with the latter were indeed in many ways striking. Both were born on the land, went to work very young with almost no education, escaped to the town and joined the proletariat, worked their way up by knowing how to operate within a major organization (the Transport Union and the Communist Party of the Soviet Union), knowing which backs to slap and which, on occasion, to stab. Both were awkward colleagues and good bosses, capable of inspiring devotion in their followers. There the analogy ends. Bevin was, as I have said, a magnanimous man, assured and self-confident. Khrushchev's shoulder retained its chip; even when he was at the head of one of the greatest Powers in history he remained the peasant suspicious of the *barin*, now transformed into the capitalist Powers of the West. His fall came after my time, and I have no contribution to make to its explanation.

Bulganin, Malenkov's successor as Prime Minister, was different again. Rubicund, with a white Imperial and quiff and little twinkling blue eyes, he radiated good temper and *bonhomie*. The American Ambassador compared him to the traditional Virginian Colonel. He was a heavy drinker, as I have recorded, and not at all ashamed of it. Once when he was Prime Minister I had to call on him to deliver a message from London, on the morning after a heavy night at which we had both been present. He asked me how I felt. I told him I was all right; how was he? 'I've got a hang-over,' he said cheerfully. One can hardly imagine a Western Prime Minister admitting this to a foreign Ambassador, but the traditional Russian attitude to heavy drinking has always been very permissive. When he first became Prime Minister he clearly made an effort to reduce his drinking, and he was very careful on his trips abroad. But at home there were occasional lapses.

All these three were typical *apparatchiki*, members of the Party apparatus who had spent their whole careers as Party officials and professional politicians. But they were not Old Bolsheviks. There was only one specimen of this almost extinct genus around in my time, and that was Molotov; all the others had been killed off in Stalin's purges. Molotov was superficially a little ridiculous, with his stammer and his pince-nez; the Foreign Office nickname for him was Aunty Moll, paired off with Uncle Joe (Stalin). He seemed ridiculous not only to us but to his colleagues. When Khrushchev and Bulganin were visiting London in 1956 they were much struck by the number of bowler hats they saw in the streets, and speculated in my hearing whether anyone they knew could ever have possessed one; they decided to their great amusement that Molotov in his youth must certainly have worn one regularly. Molotov sometimes even seemed to find himself a little ridiculous; when at some international meeting he told a lie so outrageous that everyone burst out laughing he would join in himself.

Yet with all this he was in many ways rather a formidable figure. He had been with the Party since its earliest days (he was the first editor of *Pravda*) and had lived through all its horrors, its disasters and its triumphs. He was a real believer. Though persecuted and maltreated by Stalin he genuinely mourned his death. Moreover, to say a rather old-fashioned thing, he had the instincts of a gentleman. He could be brutal and cold, but if he was entertaining a foreign Ambassador he would do so with dignity and would be careful not to embarrass him by publicly attacking his Government or by asking him to drink a toast to which the Ambassador could not subscribe. When he resigned as Foreign Minister in June 1956 most of the Ambassadors in Moscow regretted his departure; we felt that in dealing with him we were dealing with the real thing.

He was succeeded by Shepilov, whom I once described as the Ribbentrop of the régime. He was the only one of the leaders who took any part in Moscow's well-concealed café society, consisting of the sons and daughters of the leading party officials and of the marshals. He differed from most of his colleagues in another odd way; he was a head taller than most of them. It was alleged that Stalin did not wish to have men around him who were taller than himself, and certainly the Presidium of the middle fifties, all close associates of Stalin, were all under five foot six in height. Shepilov, a newer arrival, could be seen standing at the back, his large, rather melancholy, rather Roman head looming above them. He was involved with Molotov and Malenkov in the so-called 'Anti-Party Plot' against Khrushchev which emerged soon after I left, and disappeared without trace, unregretted by anyone.

Vyshinski too had been Foreign Minister in his time. He was the most odious of all the Russians with whom I was in contact. He had been prosecutor at the purge trials and had clearly enjoyed his detestable role. But as an ex-Menshevik his position was always insecure. He never rose high in the Party, and when he attended the dinner at the British Embassy I have mentioned earlier his subordinate situation was obvious; he cringed when he addressed the real leaders, and did not dare to speak without their permission.

Shepilov's successor as Foreign Minister was Gromyko. He too was a new man, an official of the Ministry and never an *apparatchik* or, in those days, of any Party status. But he was a highly efficient official by any standards, lucid, hard-working, by Soviet standards straightforward and with a prodigious memory. It was obvious that successive Soviet leaders placed great confidence in him. In spite of his somewhat lugubrious appearance he was capable of an occasional laborious joke, and Iris and I had the feeling that in different circumstances it would have been possible for us to have had a real friendship with Gromyko and his nice wife.

Two other formidable figures played a great part in our lives in those days, Mikoyan and Zhukov. Mikoyan, a brilliant, rather attractive Armenian, with the hooked nose and glittering eyes of his race, highly intelligent and subtle, was perhaps the best political tactician of them all. He had a perfect sense of timing. He seemed at one time to be particularly close to Malenkov, and his resignation from the Government just before Malenkov's fall ought to have been a signal to us that Malenkov was doomed (he seems to have played a similar role at the time of the fall of Khrushchev). He had for years presided over the retail side of the Soviet economy. This was not a conspicuous success, but the reasons for this were outside Mikoyan's control and he would probably have been a powerful large-scale retailer in any country. He would also have been a successful politician.

Zhukov was the soldier in politics. He was the most successful Soviet commander in what the Russians call 'The Great Patriotic War' and a national hero. I once watched the expression on the faces of the young soldiers composing a guard of honour that Zhukov was reviewing at Vnukovo airport; their eyes followed him with a glowing devotion. Stalin had relegated him to obscurity, but after the old dictator's death he re-emerged and became first Vice-Minister of Defence and then, when Bulganin became Prime Minister, Minister of Defence. More important, he also became a full member of the Party Presidium. He had been a member of the Party all his life but never of course an *apparatchik*, always a professional soldier. His rapid rise made some foreign observers talk of Soviet Bonapartism, but given the structure of Soviet society the most he could ever have aspired to was to be a Soviet Eisenhower, never a Soviet Napoleon, and even this modest summit was not achieved; clearly he lacked political sense, whatever his military abilities. In personal contacts he created a sense of force and vigour, but he had his brutal side;

during Khrushchev's set-to with Gomulka he said to a Western Ambassador, 'We could have crushed them [the Poles] like flies.' As he said this he clenched his huge fist in an illustrative manner, and one could see he would have enjoyed the process. He was clearly a supporter of strong action to put down the Hungarian Revolution in 1956, and he got his way over this.

There were other Party leaders who played their part in my time and whom we used to meet often enough. Voroshilov, the political soldier and a favourite of Stalin's, was fairly decrepit and played no serious part, though he was at one time the nominal Head of State. Kaganovich, reputedly Stalin's brother-in-law, the only Jew in the Presidium and (according to the Israeli Ambassador) its most virulent anti-Semite, was a heavy, rough man, who had specialized in the control of transport and heavy industry; he was a fine demagogic orator. He too was involved in the 'Anti-Party Plot'. Suslov was the Party's ideologue. A melancholy, bespectacled, schoolmasterish figure, he was sometimes thought to be the leader of a Stalinist opposition to Khrushchev. But he was too totally devoid of personal magnetism ever to aspire to the leadership, and in fact he supported Khrushchev at the time of the 'Anti-Party Plot'. Furtseva, the only woman in the Presidium, was solid, capable and seemingly warm-hearted; she headed a Parliamentary delegation to London in the summer of 1956. She was very close to Khrushchev. There were other, younger figures among the leaders, about whom we used to speculate from time to time as possible successors; Brezhnev always figured in these lists, Kosygin never. Brezhnev made an impression of vigour and vitality. Kosygin seemed a dour technocrat.

Besides their qualities as individuals the Presidium had a kind of collective personality. Miss Nancy Mitford, watching them climbing up on to Lenin's tomb, thought they looked like dreary little businessmen. Sir Osbert Sitwell, who never set eyes on them, has called them 'a committee of sabre-toothed tigers'. There is, in fact, some justice in both these apparently conflicting descriptions. Little they certainly were, and there was a businesslike, technocratic side to them. They did, at first at any rate, function as a committee. And the sabre teeth were there.

iii. Soviet Foreign Policy

I have so far been trying to set the scene and describe the cast. Now for the play. The general scenario first. Soviet foreign policy was the main theme. I wrote my first despatch about it in November 1953, a month after my arrival. This despatch was intended as background material for the Three-Power meeting at Bermuda which was about to open. The Soviet Government, I reported, were likely to adhere to their twin policies of consolidating their own extended empire and of undermining the rest of the world. They were talking of co-existence, but they visualized it as the co-existence of the snake and the rabbit. Stalin's rough and provocative methods were being abandoned, because they only strengthened the resistance to Soviet policies. Korea had been typical of these methods, and Malenkov's only significant action so far had been to liquidate the Korean conflict. Other and more subtle methods would be used, for instance infiltration into trades unions and colonial subversion. Relations with other Governments would be distant but unprovocative, and there would be a 'new look' in the relaxation of social boycotts and the encouragement of non-Communist visitors to the Soviet Union.

Coming down to more detailed questions, I said I thought that the existing division of Germany suited them better than any possible alternative. They would not be interested in security guarantees (then much in the air). They were afraid of being attacked, but this fear could not be allayed by guarantees because they would have no confidence in the word of the guaranteeing Governments. They had themselves given and broken guarantees (for instance in their attack on Poland in 1939 during the currency of a non-aggression treaty) and would not rate capitalist morality as higher than their own.

Finally I concluded that nothing we were likely to do on our own side of the Iron Curtain would provoke them to cross it. I emphasized that this applied only to what we did on our own side. I put this in another way in a later despatch, in which I said that the Russians had ceased to think they could bully us but were not likely to let us bully them. In a private letter to the Foreign

Secretary a year later I reverted to these ideas. The Russians were then conducting a violent campaign against the ratification of the Paris Agreements on the rearmament of Germany. Obviously, I said, the Russians must want to prevent ratification by all the means available. But the means were not numerous. They had no real concessions to offer. Threats must therefore be used. But here again there was nothing very terrible that they could threaten, and so the threats must be kept vague. In fact all they could do was to promise to talk if we didn't ratify, and threaten not to talk if we did. What they would do when and if we did all ratify would not necessarily bear any relation to what they had threatened to do beforehand. They were, I thought, never much troubled by consistency in matters of this kind, and their decision on their course of action after ratification would be taken in the light of their interest at the time, without reference to anything they might have said earlier. My conclusion was that in making our plans for our own organization we could and should leave Russian reactions out of account.

In an earlier letter to the Foreign Secretary written just before the Berlin Conference of Foreign Ministers in February 1954 I spelt out a little more fully my ideas on Soviet policy towards Germany. I could not believe, I wrote, that our programme for Germany, which if realized must lead to the integration of a unified Germany with the West, would ever be acceptable to the Russians. 'They *ought* to believe that a Germany integrated with a genuinely pacific West would be less dangerous to them than a floating Germany, but their minds do not work that way. In any case the choice must seem to them to be between a unified Germany integrated with the West and the Federal Republic integrated with the West, and while still hoping to avoid both they will obviously prefer the latter. In short, I do not think Molotov will go to Berlin with any hope or intention of reaching an agreement with us about Germany. I think his objective will be to pin on us the blame for dividing Germany. His further objective will probably be to drive wedges between us (United States and United Kingdom) and the French by specious-sounding "European Security" proposals.'

I never felt the need to alter significantly these early expressions of opinion. Most of the ideas I expressed seemed to me then, and seem to me now, fairly obvious truisms, and my subsequent reporting on Soviet foreign policy remained within this framework. But though these main lines remained unaltered, there was considerable skirmishing between and around them. The disappearance of Stalin created widespread expectation in the West that it would now become possible to reach some kind of settlement with Moscow, and though the nature of this settlement was never clearly thought out or defined the idea of exploratory contacts was much to the fore. For their part the Russians had their own ideas, some of which were better than others. It was a good idea to accept, as they began to do at about this time, that a State was entitled if it wished to adopt a position of neutrality. Neutrality, I reported in June 1955, though having no Marxist reality, was now seen in Moscow as a useful if temporary tactical device, and in May 1956 I even suggested that the Soviet Government might in some cases prefer the maintenance of neutral régimes to the establishment of Communist Governments which they might not be able to sustain or support and which might lead to international dangers.

But if this revised attitude to neutrality, which had been anathema to Stalin, was a good idea, others were less so. One of the oddest was Molotov's suggestion, in April 1954, that the Soviet Union might be admitted to N.A.T.O.; he implied that if her admission was refused this would be convincing proof of N.A.T.O.'s aggressive character. I used to comment on this by a parable I invented. There was once, I said, a flock of sheep which was being terrorized by a wolf, which had already eaten some of them. So they built themselves a stockade with a wall so high that the wolf could not get over it. The wolf then asked to be let inside the stockade, and when the sheep refused he said it showed what nasty aggressive animals they were. To the Foreign Office I suggested that it was a mistake to defend N.A.T.O. by alluding to the Warsaw Pact, since the implication of this was that if Moscow gave up the Warsaw Pact we could sacrifice N.A.T.O. But these sacrifices would not be equivalent. If we abandoned N.A.T.O. we should be abandoning something real. On the other hand the cohesion of the Eastern bloc depended not on a few badly drafted treaties but on the presence or imminence of the Red Army, on the communist régimes in the satellite countries and on the penetration of the satellite administration by Soviet representatives. None of this would be affected by the disappearance of the Warsaw Treaty. All this was no doubt true enough in 1954, and though the coherence of the Eastern bloc has in fact subsequently been weakened in several ways this did not come about by the abrogation of the Warsaw Treaty, which of course remains in force.

The Soviet Government was thus engaged in trying out a number of variations on its traditional foreign policy. Western policy seemed to be mainly interested, in the middle fifties, in organizing some kind of meeting with the Soviet leaders. This idea arose from public pressure, inspired by the over-simplified belief of public opinion that the leaders of the Powers, being sensible, practical men, had only to sit down together round a table for all their problems to melt away. But little serious thought was given to the nature of these problems or to acceptable solutions for them. The Russians at first eluded these suggestions, perhaps because they had themselves still to sort out their own ideas, and in my first Quarterly Report sent at the end of 1953 I noted that much of the preceding three months had been spent in endless attempts to bring the Russians to a meeting, which they had stalled; they had continued vituperation against all foreign Powers, particularly the United States, and had tried out splitting tactics. However in the end a whole series of meetings came to be arranged. There was the Berlin Conference of Foreign Ministers in February 1954, another in Vienna at the time of the signing of the Austrian Treaty in May 1955, and finally the Summit Meeting at Geneva in July 1955. All of these I attended. None of them achieved anything significant. There were also the Geneva meetings on Korea and Indo-China, which I kept away from. The position of an Ambassador at these high-level meetings was always a faintly embarrassing one. He was keen to be asked, because it enhanced his position in the capital in which he was accredited. But when he got to the meeting there was never much for him to do. The Prime Minister or Foreign Secretary would arrive from London with his own team of advisers and experts, and the Ambassador from Moscow or Paris, if allowed to come, was something of a fifth wheel in the coach. He had to be given a seat in the Conference room; there were never enough of these to go round and he kept out someone else who might have been more useful. I remember that I spent a great deal of the Geneva Summit meeting re-reading *War and Peace* in my office, and I was always glad to get back to Moscow when these meetings were over.

1955 marked the high point of the post-Stalin conference era. No one thought so at the time; there were preparations for further meetings all through 1956, but the confusions and troubles of that dangerous year, culminating at the end in Hungary and Suez, put at least a temporary stop to the process. Soviet policy remained fundamentally the same. It could be summed up by the two propositions: 'What I have is mine. What you have is everyone's.' My American colleague summarized it as 'Peace at no price'. There would be no war, but no concessions and no agreements.

iv. Khrushchev v. Malenkov

So much for the general scenario. Now for the separate acts. The first and perhaps the most dramatic of these was the struggle for Stalin's succession.

Russian history conforms to a pattern of recurrent phases. There are long, stagnant periods when an autocrat is in control. Then he dies, or is removed by assassination or otherwise, and there follows a period of uncertainty about the succession, which even under the Tsars was often unregulated. This uncertain period of transition, traditionally known as a 'Time of Troubles', lasts until a new autocrat establishes himself. It is the most interesting time for a foreign observer to find himself in Moscow, because there are differing tendencies to be observed among those competing for power, and struggles occur almost in the open, as at the moment in January 1955 when *Pravda* and *Izvestia*, the organs respectively of the Communist Party and of the Soviet Government, were publicly taking differing lines on a major issue of policy. But though highly interesting to foreign observers these transition periods are also tricky and confusing, and liable to be misinterpreted; my own arrival was in the middle of one of them, and I made a major error in reporting it, though I was in good company.

Since the establishment of the Soviet Government it has been traditional, when the autocrat dies or is removed, to talk about 'collective government'. This happened when Lenin died, it happened when Stalin died, and it happened when Khrushchev was removed; the phrase was seldom heard when these three men were in established supremacy, though there was some reality in it in Lenin's time. The 'collective government' phase after Stalin's death was chiefly directed to ensuring that no one again should have such power over his colleagues as Stalin had had. The levers of power had therefore to be distributed among various hands. Beria had to be removed because he would not surrender his total control of the secret police, which had been disagreeably evident to his colleagues in the moment of panic that followed Stalin's death. Malenkov had at first inherited from Stalin control of both the Party, as its senior Secretary, and of the Government, as Prime Minister. But after a few weeks he handed over the job of Party Secretary to Khrushchev.

This might have been thought to settle the question which Lenin once described as *'Kto kovo?'*—'Who whom?' and which he thought the principal one in political life. Stalin had achieved and held his power holding the position of Party Secretary, and had only occasionally thought it worth bothering to be Prime Minister as well. The Supremacy of the Party over the Government is well-established in the Soviet Union; the equivalent of the Court Circular, for instance, will announce that such and such a function has been attended by 'high officials of the Party and Government', always in that order. Thus when Malenkov gave up the Party to Khrushchev, remaining only Prime Minister, it might have been thought that Khrushchev was clearly 'Who' and Malenkov clearly 'Whom'. But in fact the struggle continued, and one of the counts held against Malenkov later was that he had illegitimately tried to assert the supremacy of the Government apparatus over that of the Party.

The struggle was not solely a struggle for power. Major policy questions were at issue. I put my finger on the chief of these, without quite realizing I was doing so and without getting it quite right, in the first private letter I wrote to the Foreign Secretary after my arrival. In this letter, dated November 3rd, 1953, I noted that what was going on in Moscow in the internal field was much more interesting than any of the Soviet Government's recent foreign policy moves, though there was as always in the U.S.S.R. a close connexion between the two. The Soviet Government, I said, had recently been issuing a series of immensely long decrees, the main object of which was to increase the production of consumption goods, from food to television sets, and to improve the means of distributing and selling them. All these decrees involved modification of the current five-year plan in the direction of increasing consumption. Now obviously the five-year plan was intended to provide for the full use of all the industrial capacity and manpower of the country, and the increase of consumption goods must therefore be at the expense of something else. It was interesting to speculate of what.

One class of project which I thought, rightly as it turned out, might well, to judge from the deafening silence that surrounded it, prove to have been dropped, was Stalin's rather megalomaniac schemes for changing the face of nature by altering the course of rivers and by re-afforestation. But this alone would clearly not provide the necessary resources, and I wondered whether the cuts might not be falling on the armaments industry, and perhaps even on the armed forces themselves. I went on to suggest that if this were so, if the Russians were going to concentrate on raising the standard of living and to bother less about armaments, we might be in some danger of getting ready as usual for the wrong war; the real danger to the West might not be a military one but the attractions of a prosperous and successful Communism. I added, however, that to bring China along in this process would be beyond the powers even of Russia's immense resources, and that it would surely impose a considerable strain on Sino-Soviet relations if the Russians were to concentrate on their own self-improvement, leaving the Chinese much where they were.

The remark about the Chinese was moderately far-sighted for 1953. But on the rest I had missed the main point. What was to suffer to provide more consumption goods was not so much the armed forces as heavy industry. Now the supremacy of heavy industry over the consumption goods industry had always been a cardinal point in Communist Party doctrine, and it was on this issue, with some supplementary disputes about agriculture, then as always in crisis, that the Malenkov–Khrushchev battle was to be fought.

For a long time, as my reports show, I was reluctant to believe that this battle was being fought at all. This was indeed the general view of foreign observers in Moscow. We were all so conditioned to regarding the Soviet State as a monolith that we could not believe that behind its solid exterior an intense struggle was being carried on. Besides, the exterior was solid indeed. The revolution was a palace revolution, fought out behind firmly closed and heavily curtained doors; the sound of the struggle was muffled, and those outside could hear and see little of it. Thus in March 1954, a year after Stalin's death, I wrote that the Presidium was 'an efficient and harmonious team'. In August of the same year I noted that at the dinner for the Labour Party delegation Malenkov and Khrushchev seemed on better terms than all the rest, though I guarded myself by adding that this would be more convincing if we had not had the earlier example of the observed intimacy between Malenkov and Beria. At the end of December I reported that Khrushchev was becoming more of a public figure than Malenkov, but I said I thought rivalry between them was not the explanation, and in January 1955 I still expected that the Presidium's unity would survive and that there would be some kind of division of labour between Malenkov and Khrushchev.

On February 8th I was sitting with other Ambassadors in the diplomatic tribune of the Supreme Soviet (the rather unconvincing Russian equivalent of Parliament) when the chairman, in a rapid gabble, read Malenkov's letter of resignation. I could not follow it all, and said to John Morgan who was standing behind me, 'Did I hear what I thought I heard?' He confirmed that I had, and we hurried back to the Embassy to send off reports. In one of these I admitted that Malenkov's resignation had taken everyone by surprise, 'myself not least', and speculated rather absurdly that Khrushchev might have wished Malenkov to carry on but that Malenkov had refused. I long remained reluctant to believe that

Malenkov was finished. As late as the end of 1956 I was reporting that ever since his resignation as Prime Minister Malenkov had looked more and more like the coming man. It must be remembered that all this time he remained a member of the Presidium, essentially the most important body in the Soviet Union; he was ten years younger than Khrushchev and unquestionably more intelligent, and he had in the eyes of many Russians what was still the advantage of having been Stalin's closest associate and of resembling him most nearly. It was not until his final removal after the leading part he took, with Molotov and Kaganovich, in the 'Anti-Party Plot' against Khrushchev in the summer of 1957, after my departure, that all hope of a Malenkov comeback disappeared.

It was odd that, like most other observers of the Moscow scene, I should have been so reluctant to believe that Malenkov was on the way out. To some extent the wish was father to the thought. It was not that any of us particularly liked Malenkov. But we thought it would be easier to do business with him than with Khrushchev, of whose character we had formed, as I have recorded earlier, a mistaken impression. Moreover in the controversies that divided the two men Western interests seemed to be on Malenkov's side. A Russia concentrating on improving its own standards of living seemed preferable to one that was building up its military strength through the development of heavy industry. Malenkov seemed to represent the new technocratic forces growing up in Soviet society, which were more likely to want normal relations with the rest of the world than the Party doctrinaires for whom Khrushchev was battling. Furthermore Malenkov in March of 1954 had said that a world war would ruin world civilization. For this obvious truism he was subsequently taken to task by the Party, whose official doctrine at the time was that another war would ruin only capitalism, a view now probably confined to the Chinese Communist Party; and in this controversy we were all, for obvious reasons, once more on Malenkov's side. When he resigned I reported that from now on we could not count on the patience and caution that were characteristic of the Malenkov era, and it was no doubt our belief in the seriousness of this loss that made us so reluctant to admit that it had really occurred. What we did not realize was that, as so often before in Soviet history, the victor was to take over almost all the policies for which he had been criticizing his defeated rival.

v. The Twentieth Party Congress

Even after Malenkov's resignation Khrushchev's sole autocracy was not established. He himself proposed Bulganin for Malenkov's successor as Prime Minister, and for a long time a form of government prevailed which, though not exactly collective since its elements were warring against one another, was not a one-man dictatorship either.

A most important landmark along this road was the Twentieth Party Congress held in February 1956, the first since Stalin's death. This Congress was indeed a turning-point in the history of the Soviet Union, both internally and in its external relations. Internally this is obvious enough, but it should be noted that at this Congress the seeds were sown from which grew the Polish dispute, the Hungarian Revolution, and ultimately the breach with China. To the non-Communist world, and indeed to most Communists, the most important aspect of the Congress was that it was the scene of the first official denunciations of Stalin, both in the published speeches of Mikoyan and others and in Khrushchev's famous 'secret' speech. I remember once telling Khrushchev and Bulganin at some Kremlin reception that in my reports to the Foreign Office I had said that the doctrinal innovations of the Congress were ultimately more important than anything that had been said there about Stalin. They made approving noises, and perhaps in the long run I was right; but certainly the short-run effects of de-Stalinization were pretty far reaching, probably much more so than its authors had intended or expected.

The reasons for de-Stalinization were clear enough. Khrushchev and his associates were trying to modernize the Soviet State and to free it from the ossified rigidity into which Stalin had fixed it. But obviously this process could not succeed if those hostile to it could at any time appeal to Stalin's actions and writings as holy writ. It was necessary to demolish Stalin's moral authority if his policies were to be repudiated, and this was effectively done at the Twentieth Party Congress. But the psychologically disruptive effects of this had perhaps not been foreseen. The man whom every Soviet citizen for decades and every Eastern European for years had been taught to revere as an all-wise, benevolent hero was suddenly revealed as an inefficient monster. The general respect for Soviet authority, both in the Soviet Union itself and in the satellites, was more diminished in the process than had been calculated, and the rest of 1956 was to show the consequences of this.

The Congress's doctrinal innovations were nevertheless very important. They were in essence two. The first was the repudiation of Lenin's doctrine that war between the capitalist and the Communist countries was ultimately inevitable. The second was the announcement that Socialism or Communism could in certain circumstances be established in a bourgeois State constitutionally, by Parliamentary means for instance, and that a violent revolution was not a necessary antecedent though it might still be necessary in certain cases. These two changes in doctrine were clearly not brought about by any process of rigorous intellectual analysis. They were introduced because the doctrines they replaced were proving practically inconvenient for the conduct of Soviet policy. To proclaim the inevitability of war in an atomic age was likely to render the Soviet Government unpopular. And it was a useful weapon against Communist Parties in bourgeois countries to be able to show that they were dedicated to unconstitutional processes and to the overthrow of the existing order by violence. These changes were therefore of a strictly practical kind, and as such typical of Khrushchev's approach to doctrinal matters. Khrushchev did not aspire, as Stalin did, to rewrite holy writ himself; he accepted it as given, except where it was practically inconvenient, and then he took steps to have it altered.

Apart from commenting on particular events at the Congress I devoted some time in my reports to speculating about the kind of country that we could expect to see emerging as a result of the policy lines the Congress had laid down. It was clearly of the utmost importance to the rest of the world to know how the Soviet Union under its new masters was going to develop. The only hope for a peaceful world, I thought, was that Communism

in the Soviet Union should settle down and change from an expanding to a conservative force. There were no other possibilities.
The régime would not collapse. It could not be overthrown except
by war, which was unthinkable. Genuine co-existence with
expanding Marxism was impossible.

What then could we expect the Soviet Union, as refashioned
by the Twentieth Party Congress, to be like? I thought there
would be no transition to full Communism, but impressive
technological development and material progress. There would
be a rigid but not unduly harsh political framework. Opposition
would not be allowed, but the asperities of the police-state would
be softened. Collective leadership, I believed, would continue in
some form. There were no candidates for a dictatorship of the old
kind. Khrushchev was unsuited by temperament for this and too
old to have time to establish himself (he was then sixty-two); but
he was strong enough to be able to keep everyone else out.

I do not seem, in these reports, to have answered my own
question whether Russia after the Congress was or was not
settling down into a process of 'embourgeoisement'. One may
continue to hope so, but the régime in Russia has always been a
baffling, Protean thing. What is it really like? Let an abler pen
than mine describe it first.

This pitiful fate of a country held by an evil spell, suffering
from an awful visitation for which the responsibility cannot be
traced either to her sins or her follies, has made Russia as a
nation so difficult to understand by Europe. From the very
first ghastly dawn of her existence as a State she had to breathe
the atmosphere of despotism; she found nothing but the
arbitrary will of an obscure autocrat at the beginning and end
of her organization. Hence arises her impenetrability to whatever is true in Western thought. Western thought, when it
crosses her frontier, falls under the spell of her autocracy and
becomes a noxious parody of itself. Hence the contradictions,
the riddles of her national life, which are looked upon with
such curiosity by the rest of the world. The curse had entered
her very soul; autocracy, and nothing else in the world, has
moulded her institutions, and with the poison of slavery

5*

drugged the national temperament into the apathy of a hopeless fatalism. It seems to have gone into the blood, tainting every mental activity in its source by a half-mystical, insensate fascinating assertion of purity and holiness. The Government of Holy Russia, arrogating to itself the supreme power to torment and slaughter the bodies of its subjects like a God-sent scourge, has been most cruel to those whom it allowed to live under the shadow of its dispensations. The worst crime against humanity of that system we behold now crouching at bay behind vast heaps of mangled corpses is the ruthless destruction of innumerable minds. The greatest horror of the world—madness—walked faithfully in its train. Some of the best intellects of Russia, after struggling in vain against the spell, ended by throwing themselves at the feet of that hopeless despotism as a giddy man leaps into an abyss. An attentive survey of Russia's literature, of her Church, of her administration and the crosscurrents of her thought, must end in the verdict that the Russia of today has not the right to give her voice on a single question touching the future of humanity, because from the very inception of her being the brutal destruction of dignity, of truth, of rectitude, of all that is faithful in human nature has been made the imperative condition of her existence.

This was written by Joseph Conrad in 1905.* Conrad, as a Pole, was prejudiced; but he was near to Russia and aware of its problems and its impact on its neighbours, and much of what he writes is relevant now. His allusion to the way in which Russia transforms Western ideas is strongly applicable to the present situation of Communism; it is very unlikely that Karl Marx (that notorious Russophobe) or Engels would recognize or acknowledge as their own the forms which their doctrines have assumed in the Soviet Union. Byzantine complications have distorted Western ideas of relative clarity, and Western attempts to understand the result are often defeated.

We used at the British Embassy to spend a good deal of time trying to answer the question where power resided in the Soviet

* See his essay 'Autocracy and War', republished in 'Notes on Life and Letters'.

Union. Here we come back to H. W. B. Joseph's question about the rule of law. In a State where this rule prevails the mechanisms of power are fairly easy to detect. A British Government that loses its majority in Parliament resigns. An American President who is defeated in an election makes way for his successor. But how does power transmit itself in Russia? If you are Prime Minister and order the arrest of the head of the secret police, may he not arrest you? Of course ultimate physical power there, as in any State, lies with the armed forces (as Belloc so succinctly put it: 'Whatever happens we have got The Maxim gun, and they have not'). But in civilized States the armed forces are in subjection to the civil power, and this is generally so in Russia. There is not in Russia, as there is in Germany, Spain or Latin America, any tradition of intervention by the army as such in politics, though individual army officers have played political roles. If the political leaders are in conflict and disarray the Army's allegiance is important and may be decisive, as it was when Zhukov's support for Khrushchev at the time of the 'Anti-Party Plot' secured his victory. But once Khrushchev's victory was secure and the political leadership was united again, Khrushchev had no difficulty at all in eliminating Zhukov, national hero though he was, from all political influence and from his military command. In normal times, at least, power must reside elsewhere.

In Stalin's time it lay in various places, and he maintained his autocracy by deploying one sector of power against another, the secret police against the Army against the Party against the Government and so on. One of the first acts of his successors was to eliminate the secret police as a source of power, since it had in the past proved too dangerous to themselves (this too was accomplished with the help of the Army). The Khrushchev–Malenkov dispute settled for good and all the supremacy of the Party over the Government. So power must reside somewhere within the Party. For day-to-day purposes it must lie between the Presidium and the Secretariat, but these bodies were clearly too small and unrepresentative for their verdicts to be accepted as final in case of a dispute. Constitutionally the Party Congress was supreme, but this only met at intervals of several years and was clearly not the effective sovereign body. Our conclusion was that power really lay with the Central Committee, which emanates from the Congress and of which the Presidium is itself an emanation. We thought that a vote there would be accepted as decisive. We were interested to find that the American Embassy, which had been independently carrying out a similar analysis, had come to the same conclusion. Our joint conclusion was strikingly confirmed at the time of the 'Anti-Party Plot' when Khrushchev, having been put in a minority in the Presidium, was able with Zhukov's help to get together a meeting of the Central Committee. This meeting supported him, whereupon his opponents gave up the struggle. It seems to have been the case that when Khrushchev himself was overthrown it was again the Central Committee's verdict that was accepted as final.

However the elucidation of this technical point, though it suggests the embryonic growth of something resembling the rule of law in Russia, does not really help us to determine the real nature of the Soviet régime. One can only say that the dark forces so graphically described by Conrad, which in Stalin's time were given their head, now seem to be in retreat. The secret police are curbed, and can hardly escape again from this curb. Stalin's successors are trying to repudiate their horrifying inheritance, and have started a slow march towards a more civilized State. There may be pauses and even slight retreats on this march, but its general direction cannot now be reversed. The whole world ought to be grateful to Malenkov and Khrushchev, in their different ways, for having started to move the old colossus slowly up the hill towards the light.

vi. Bulganin and Khrushchev in England

Once Khrushchev had established himself in power he began to show a marked interest in foreign affairs. This took the practical form of wishing to acquaint himself at first hand with foreigners, and then with their countries. Stalin had remained immured within the Kremlin; even the exigencies of wartime consultation never lured him further than Tehran. But Khrushchev, out of curiosity, out of a desire to learn, out of a desire to impress, began to travel. England would perhaps not have stood first in his list.

The foreign country in which the majority of Russians, and perhaps the Soviet Government, are most interested is America. It is the goal they are constantly being urged, or urging themselves, to 'catch up and overtake'. They share many tastes with it, love of gadgets, technology, massive scale. Khrushchev, in his intoxicated speech in the park which I have described in the first section of this chapter, revealed not only his own but his country's estimate of what really matters in the world. In spite of appearances America is their favourite foreign country.

England has never occupied this position, though Anglomania was once endemic in the aristocracy of St. Petersburg. But in the nineteenth century we were the Russian Empire's greatest rival, and at the time of the Revolution and later we were foolish enough to lead the forces of intervention. So we have not been very popular. But we were probably, in my time in Moscow, the capitalist country to which most attention was paid after America. This led to a brisk interchange of delegations, artistic manifestations, and so on. The political temperature rose and fell. The Anglo-Soviet Treaty was denounced by the Russians in May 1955 (quite illegally since there was no provision for ending it before 1962) as part of their campaign against German rearmament. But after the Geneva Summit meeting in July of that year a slightly chequered honeymoon period set in, culminating in the visit which Bulganin and Khrushchev paid to the United Kingdom in April 1956. There followed an afterglow, ultimately extinguished by the events of that disastrous autumn.

The visit to England arose, so far as I know, in the following manner. Sir Anthony Eden had invited me to spend a night at Chequers before the Geneva Summit meeting. After we had discussed probable Russian attitudes to the Geneva agenda he asked me whether they were likely to raise any specifically Anglo-Soviet questions. I said they were certain to invite him to visit Moscow. He asked me what I thought he should say to that, and I suggested that he should remind them that there had been many official British visits to Moscow during the war, which had never been repaid, and that he might counter-invite them to London. I knew that Khrushchev was anxious to enlarge his horizons, and I thought this would be one good way of doing it. Sir Anthony liked the idea, and when the inevitable invitation to Moscow was issued at Geneva he made the suggested counter-proposal, which the Russians in due course accepted for the following April.

In the interval which elapsed before April came round I began to wonder whether this had been such a good idea after all. In December Bulganin and Khrushchev went off to India, where they made a number of violent anti-colonialist speeches, denouncing British imperialism to not particularly receptive audiences. But this was smoothed over and forgotten, and it soon became clear that the visit was going to take place all right. I myself was invited to appear on Soviet television (the first Ambassador to do so) to speak about the visit, a rather indifferent exhibition of British art, drawn entirely from Russian sources, was arranged, and at a Kremlin reception in March Bulganin, Khrushchev and Malenkov lined up behind each other, saying they were queueing for a visit to England. Malenkov went off there at the end of that month as head of a delegation from the electricity industry (he was then Minister of Electric Power Stations, the rather incongruous post to which he had been demoted from being Prime Minister). I went to meet him on his return, a rather hair-raising experience. It was a blustery, overcast day, and his TU-104, the then very new Soviet jet air-liner, appeared out of the clouds at Vnukovo, failed to land and took off again into the overcast. My Air Attaché who was with me told me the aircraft could not have fuel for more than five minutes' flying time left, and we were worried for Malenkov's safety as well as for that of our Assistant Air Attaché who was on board (the latter told us later he was sure a crash was imminent and had taken up an appropriate position in the aircraft). We kept our anxieties from Malenkov's wife and daughter, who were standing with us, and in due course the aircraft came round again and landed safely, its parachute brakes trailing. Malenkov appeared beaming at the top of the steps and invited us on board to look at the new aircraft. Outside, its lines were splendidly smooth and modern; inside, it was furnished, as Miss Nancy Mitford said of another Soviet plane, like a cottage, with a good deal of red plush and china figurines in glass cases.

Whether because this alarming experience had been reported

to them or for other reasons, Bulganin and Khrushchev chose to go to England in a cruiser. I had flown home earlier, since it had been decided that I was to accompany them throughout their visit. The programme that had been designed for them was not one I should have chosen myself; it took them to a number of historical and beautiful places, but neither of them had any visual sense or any interest in history, and they saw little of the modern industrial or agricultural areas in which Khrushchev at least would have been really interested and by which they might have been impressed. There seems to have been some idea that if they got among the people at all they would make rabble-rousing speeches of the kind they had permitted themselves in India, and that this might lead to incidents.

In point of fact their reception must have been something of a surprise to them. This was their first visit to an industrialized capitalist country, and their stereotypes told them that while the Government would be hostile the people would greet them as the beloved representatives of the Workers' State. But the opposite occurred; the Government was hospitable and welcoming, while the popular reception was, to put it mildly, mixed. Once when we were driving together in our huge hired car Khrushchev said to me, 'What is that oo, oo noise they make?'

'It isn't oo, oo,' I said, 'it's boo, boo.'

'What does it mean?'

'It doesn't mean anything, it's just a noise.'

'But does it indicate disapproval?' he persisted.

I thought it was no good trying to conceal this, and admitted that it did. 'Well, next time they do that to me I shall do it back to them,' he said, and for the rest of that drive he was saying 'boo, boo' most of the way.

On the whole, however, both he and Bulganin studiously, and no doubt as the result of a deliberate policy, refrained throughout the visit from comment, unfavourable or otherwise, on what they saw and heard. I felt that they were under considerable strain throughout (the only time they seemed really relaxed, oddly enough, was at a tea-party in Holyroodhouse attended by every duke and duchess in Scotland). When they left I accompanied them down to Portsmouth and they invited me on board their

cruiser for a drink. One sensed their relief at being back in a
Russian atmosphere as they called for the vodka and the Armenian
brandy.

There had been many bizarre incidents before that final conclusion. Some of the oddest were at Oxford. The police arrangements there broke down almost entirely, and the streets were
blocked from side to side with cheerful crowds singing 'Poor old
Joe', an allusion to their late master which was entirely lost on
Bulganin and Khrushchev who did not know the tune and would
not have recognized Stalin under the sobriquet of Joe. The police
inspector in charge told me that he could not answer for their
safety if they went to Christ Church as planned, so I took it upon
myself to cancel the visit there; I have always regretted this
decision since I learnt subsequently that it had been planned that as
they entered Tom Gate four undergraduates, all disguised as
Stalin, would appear at each corner of Tom Quad. Instead they
went straight to New College where, since the then Warden was
Vice-Chancellor, they were to be principally entertained. We
somehow arrived before the Warden, and to fill in time I took
them up to see the not very luxurious room in the Garden Quadrangle which I had occupied as an undergraduate. 'I wish I had
had a room like this when I was a student,' said Khrushchev a
little wistfully. In the Chapel Khrushchev's derogatory remarks
about Epstein's statue of Lazarus which stands there were overheard by a journalist, who reported them in his paper. Next day
the Warden of New College got a telegram from Epstein saying,
'Tell your guest to keep off art criticism, which he does not
understand, and stick to his own business, which is murder.'
There is no doubt that the statue made a deep impression on
Khrushchev. Next morning when Iris and I met him in the foyer
of Claridge's he said to her, 'Did you sleep well last night?' She
replied that she had and asked him how his night had been. 'I had
nightmares from that terrible statue at Oxford,' he said. This is,
I suppose, at least evidence that his dislike of modern art (in
which category he undoubtedly included Epstein) was genuine
and not a mere matter of ideology.

After leaving New College Chapel Bulganin and Khrushchev
went up the stairs to Hall, while I remained behind for a moment

in the Front Quadrangle to fix up with Isaiah and Aline Berlin
about their forthcoming visit to us in Moscow. As I was chatting
with them on the lawn I heard a loud bang and saw a cloud of
smoke issuing from the Hall stairs. I had always been slightly
nervous of an incident of this kind, and felt they might think it
sinister that it should have happened on what was practically the
first occasion I had left their side. I hurried over, but it was harmless enough, only a thunder flash, and we went on up into the
Hall. It was the first day of term, and the undergraduates were
writing Collections in a silence that seemed to me unnatural until
I saw that here too something odd was going on. A large, gaudy
poster had been stuck into the frame of the Founder's portrait.
David Eccles and I were examining this and had just discovered
that it portrayed Stalin surrounded by his closest associates when
up came Khrushchev. He identified the figures in the poster,
genially enough; 'That's me, and there's Comrade Molotov, and
there's Comrade Kaganovich, and there's Comrade . . . er . . .
and there's Comrade Voroshilov.' 'Comrade er' was Beria.

The more serious side of the visit has been described in Sir
Anthony Eden's Memoirs, and I have nothing to add to his
account of the discussions at 10 Downing Street and Chequers.
These were all very amiable in tone, though there were ominous
rumblings when the subject of Egypt and Middle East oil came
up. The meeting with the Labour Party was less agreeable.
Khrushchev went to this without me. I had heard that there had
been rows, and rather maliciously asked him next morning how it
had gone. 'It couldn't have gone worse,' he replied. 'That's what
happens when you go out without me,' I told him. It was not
only George Brown who got across him. A day later, Aneurin
Bevan, as we walked together out of the Speaker's lunch where
Khrushchev had again shown himself in an aggressive mood,
kept repeating, 'He's an impossible man, an impossible man.'
There is no doubt that the dislike was reciprocated; when we got
back to Moscow Khrushchev said to me, 'Bulganin can vote
Labour if he likes but I'm going to vote Conservative.'

The Conservative leaders had clearly made a favourable impression on Khrushchev. At a Kremlin Party for the Shah in July,
Khrushchev said to me that though we had our differences and

arguments he thought our relations were now in a much better condition, and he added, 'I have great confidence in Eden, I have great confidence in Selwyn Lloyd, and I have great confidence in Butler; I am sure they are all anxious for peace, and I think we are beginning to understand each other.' Nor was it only to me that he was speaking in this way; the Indian Ambassador told me that at the same party he had had some conversation with Bulganin and Khrushchev about Algeria, in the course of which they contrasted French policy there with our policy in India and had said they had noticed in India how good our relations with the Indian Government and people were as a result of the manner in which we had left India; Bulganin had gone on to pay a glowing personal tribute to Sir Anthony Eden. A return visit by the Prime Minister and the Foreign Secretary was planned for the following April. But all this was swept away by the terrible events which followed in Eastern Europe and the Middle East.

vii. Hungary and Suez

At the beginning of October 1956, before returning to Moscow after my summer leave, I went to see a very senior Foreign Office official and asked him about the Government's policy towards Egypt. I could quite understand, I said, the attempts that were then being made, by conferences and by diplomacy, to oblige Nasser to disgorge the Suez Canal, which he had nationalized two months before. But these attempts to secure restitution by peaceful means might fail; did we then intend to use force to secure control of the Canal?

'That I can't tell you,' replied the Under-Secretary.

At the time I took this somewhat ambiguous reply to mean that he did not know the answer. I have since wondered whether he meant that he knew the answer but was not allowed to tell me.

When I got back to Moscow a few days later I found that few people there were thinking much about the Middle East. All attention was on Eastern Europe, where the process of de-Stalinization started by the Twentieth Party Congress was proving a rough one. The moral authority, such as it was, of the Stalinist régimes in the East European satellites had been severely shaken by the revelations about Stalin's real character, and some of them would clearly have to be replaced. It had been officially admitted, in the communiqué after Tito's meeting with Khrushchev in June, that there could be 'different roads to Socialism'. There had been riots in Poland in the same month, and in July Rákosi, the very Stalinist Party boss in Hungary, had been removed from the post of Party Secretary. On October 21st Gomulka, a strongly anti-Stalinist Communist, came to power in Poland despite very strong Soviet pressure, in the course of which military action was threatened (and, as I have recorded, strongly advocated by Marshal Zhukov and the army). The Gomulka solution was that Poland should remain in the Warsaw Pact, i.e. in close alliance with Moscow, but should be allowed free control of its own internal affairs provided always that this control was Communist. Rokosovsky, the former Soviet Marshal who had become Polish Minister of Defence and symbolized Soviet interference in Polish internal affairs, was dismissed and returned to Russia. In all this the Poles showed a most uncharacteristic restraint; they themselves were conscious of this, and said that the Hungarians were behaving like Poles and the Poles like Czechs (the Poles have always despised the Czechs for their prudent and calculating natures). No doubt the explanation lies to some extent in the personal characters of the anti-Stalinist Communist leaders in the two countries. Gomulka was a much stronger man than Nagy. And perhaps it is also relevant, in these two strongly Catholic countries, that Cardinal Wyszinsky in Poland was a much more intelligent man than Cardinal Mindszenty in Hungary.

For events in Hungary, as we all know, followed a very different and much more catastrophic course. In July, when Rákosi was removed, the Hungarians would have been delighted if anyone had offered them a Gomulka-type solution (and it is in fact the situation which, after so much bloodshed and anguish, they have now achieved under Kadar). But Rákosi was replaced at first not by Nagy but by Gerö, an ineffective Stalinist instead of an effective one, and pressure grew up, powerfully reinforced by the example of Poland. Fighting broke out in Budapest on October 23rd; the Hungarian Government asked for Soviet help, but Nagy was brought to power and on October 30th the Soviet troops were withdrawn from the Hungarian capital. The Soviet Government issued on the same day an important statement on their policy towards the satellite countries in general, which seemed to foreshadow a move towards something like Dominion status for all of them. There was to be equality in economic matters, Soviet 'advisers' would be withdrawn, and the presence of Soviet troops would be 'examined'; but the People's Democracies, as they were called, were to remain in the Warsaw Pact and 'to maintain the Socialist structures of their States'.

This was enough for Gomulka, and it would probably have been enough for Nagy if he had got it in time. But other events and pressures now intervened. On October 29th the Israelis invaded Egypt. On the evening of October 30th, at a Kremlin reception for the Prime Minister of Afghanistan, Molotov was saying to every Ambassador who spoke to him that Britain and France were behind the Israeli invasion. The Ambassadors duly passed this on to me, and I assured them that Molotov was wrong; the matter was bound to come to the Security Council, and there I was certain they would find us voting for measures to restrain Israeli aggression, much as we might dislike doing so in view of the way in which Nasser had been behaving. When I returned to the Embassy I found that in my absence the text of the Anglo-French ultimatum to Egypt and Israel had just arrived. As I read it I could not believe my eyes; I even began to wonder if I had drunk too much at the Kremlin. I felt quite bewildered. The action we were taking seemed to me flatly contrary to all that I knew, or thought I knew, about British policy, as my reaction to Molotov's insinuations had showed. I believed that we were strongly opposed to the use of force to obtain national ends, and here we were condoning such use (even though by a friend against an enemy) and apparently preparing to use it ourselves. We were too, it seemed to me, about to use it for a futile purpose. My father more than thirty years before had written scathingly of those who kept pressing for 'a firm hand in Egypt and the maintenance of British prestige' that 'we shall best maintain our prestige by following a consistent policy and keeping our promises; and what is the good of a firm hand in seizing something which you have already decided you do not want?' These remarks seemed to me perfectly apposite to the policy we were now pursuing. Moreover I was already beginning to suspect that we were in breach of what I had always thought another cardinal principle of our policy, to keep in step with the Americans. But obviously there was nothing I could do about it that night, so I went up to bed.

However my troubles were not then at an end. Iris and I had always acted on the assumption that our bedroom was microphoned. I knew that she would feel as I did if I told her about the ultimatum, and we might then be betrayed into saying things about our Government's policy that we should not wish the Russians to hear. So I said nothing to her that evening. But I lay awake most of the night wondering, not for the last time during this crisis, whether I ought not to send in my resignation.

Next morning I had powerful confirmation that we were out of step with the Americans. There was a tiresome custom at Moscow that when a distinguished visitor arrived all the Ambassadors met him at the airport. This morning it was the President of Syria, and the American Ambassador, as we waited on the tarmac, expressed to me his anger and astonishment at our action at Suez. He asked me if I had any idea what my Government was up to, and I was obliged to tell him I had none at all. He was particularly perturbed because at this moment we were all aware that there was a certain hesitation and perhaps division in the Soviet Government about what to do next in Hungary, and the Ambassador feared that our action at Suez might influence this decision in the wrong direction. All the other N.A.T.O. Ambassadors (except the new French Ambassador, Maurice Dejean, who was a strong supporter of Suez) were equally puzzled and angry.

This was the period when Hungary was, briefly and intoxicatingly, free. I sent an optimistic telegram to the Foreign Office that day, saying I thought that the declaration of October 30th meant that the Soviet Government had decided not to use their troops to suppress the Hungarian Revolution or in the satellites generally, and on November 2nd Bulganin told the American Ambassador that no more Soviet troops were being sent to Hungary. The Ambassador did not believe him, and he was quite right. Unfortunately freedom had proved too intoxicating to the

Hungarians, and Nagy had moved on, reluctantly perhaps, past the Gomulka formula; he had demanded the withdrawal of all Soviet troops, denounced the Warsaw Pact and proclaimed the holding of elections in which non-Communist Parties would be allowed to participate.

Meanwhile the Western Alliance was in total dissarray. This had its partly painful, partly ridiculous repercussions in Moscow. The Syrian Embassy gave a reception for their President on November 2nd. The French Ambassador and I, who had been invited some time before to this reception, inquired through the Persian Ambassador whether our presence would still be welcome and were encouraged to attend. It was a highly embarrassing occasion. Many of our colleagues were unwilling to be seen talking to us, and it was particularly painful for us to be unable to speak to the Egyptian Ambassador, Mohamed Elkony, and his charming wife, who had become very close friends (and I am glad to say have remained so in spite of everything). However, comic relief was provided by the behaviour of a Latin Ambassador, a man of unattractive habits, who took it upon himself to be censorious on this occasion. Iris's diary records that at this party 'he shook my hand instead of kissing it. I have been trying to achieve this for years and feel that he is the last person, both personally and because of his country's role in the war, to have any right to condemn anything, so that we were amused and cheered up'. By this time she and I had been able, during a walk in the open air, to discuss freely what was going on in Egypt, and found that as I expected we were united in detesting it.

The next day the Bohlens and the John Gunthers (he was in Moscow getting material for his *Inside Russia Today*) dined with us at the Embassy. We were all depressed at the news that the Russians had taken the fateful decision to send their troops back to Budapest, and by the following day (November 4th) it was clear that Hungary was doomed, though fighting continued for several more days. At this time Soviet Embassies all over Europe were becoming the object of hostile demonstrations, and the Soviet Government thought it ought to do something to redress the balance. The Russian people were unlikely to do anything on their own. They were much confused by all these events, and there was current in Moscow a symbolic story of the Soviet soldier sent to Budapest who thought the Danube was the Suez Canal. But the Soviet Government does not believe in leaving matters of this kind to chance or to the spontaneous reactions of its people, and so on November 5th a small and rather ineffective demonstration was organized against the British, French and Israeli Embassies. The entrance gates at our Embassy were closed and no attempt was made to break through them, though posters were stuck on the walls and the railings.

That night, after I had gone to bed, I was woken up and summoned to the Ministry of Foreign Affairs, to become the personal recipient of the first of Khrushchev's rocket-rattling threats. This was in the form of a note handed to me by Shepilov, the Minister of Foreign Affairs, containing the text of a letter from Bulganin to the Prime Minister. After references to the 'aggressive, brigandly war against the Arab peoples' and to attempts to restore 'the régime of colonial slavery which the people had overthrown', came the rocket rattling:

> 'What would have been the position of Britain if she had been attacked by stronger Powers, with all kinds of modern offensive weapons at their disposal? And remember that such countries at the present time need not even send their naval and air forces to British shores, but could use other means, such as rocket techniques. If rocket weapons were used against Britain and France, you would no doubt call this a barbarous act . . .
>
> 'I appeal to you, to Parliament, to the Labour Party, to the Trade Unions, to the whole British people: stop armed aggression and cease bloodshed. The war in Egypt can spread to other countries and grow into a Third World War . . . We are filled with determination to use force to crush the aggressors and to restore peace in the East.
>
> 'We hope that at this critical moment you will show the necessary prudence and will draw from this the appropriate conclusions.'

After I had read this stuff through (there was a lot more of it) I said to Shepilov that it called for no comment from me at this stage. Shepilov replied brusquely that he did not expect comment;

he only asked me to pass it on. It was in fact obvious why he had sent for me at that unearthly hour; the message was published several hours before it reached the Prime Minister, even though I had sent it on by urgent diplomatic wireless the moment I got back to the Embassy, and it is clear enough from its text that its intention was not to persuade the Prime Minister but to put pressure on him, or at least to appear to be doing so. I have never known for certain how great a part it played in the decision to call off the Suez operation, which was in fact taken the following morning. Personally I later came to believe that this decision was taken on other grounds, and moreover that the Russians when they sent their letter knew that our collapse was inevitable and imminent and cashed in on this by delivering threats they were sure they would never have to carry out, thus enabling themselves to pose as the saviours of the Arabs. Whether this was true or not it worked beautifully in the Arab world, as I found on a visit to the Middle East a year later. Everyone there was certain that it was Khrushchev's rocket threat that had stopped us, and the effect of this on British and Russian prestige in the Middle East can well be imagined.

I did not of course know on the morning of November 6th that a decision to stop the operation was imminent. Early that morning I sent the Foreign Office my views on Bulganin's letter and the situation which it created. There was, I said, an element of bullying bluff in it. But I was afraid that the Soviet Government were working themselves up into a very ugly mood (as I wrote this the Embassy was being besieged by organized demonstrators). I thought they might intend, after the inevitable rejection of a proposal they had just made to the Americans for joint action against us and the French, to take some violent independent action against our forces in the Middle East (I had in mind, though I did not say so, action against our sea communication in the Mediterranean by submarine or aircraft which might well be unidentifiable). I therefore said I thought it was vitally necessary to get into step with the United States again immediately; 'only clear and immediate proof of this will stop these people from committing dangerous acts of folly.'

Later that morning I telegraphed again urging that we should reply the same day, if only because the following day, November 7th, was a Soviet holiday when all the leading men would be unavailable. I suggested that our reply ought to take the following lines:

(a) We should say that the Prime Minister's first reaction had been to instruct me to return the note as entirely unacceptable, but that one more attempt at reasoning must be made.

(b) Bulganin's letter had not mentioned the primary objective of the Anglo-French action, which was to separate the combatants and stop the fighting. This had been achieved.

(c) The Canadian proposal for United Nations action should be adopted. If this occurred British and French forces would withdraw. A peaceful solution would then be in sight if the Soviet Government did not confuse the issue by precipitate action.

(d) Our willingness to withdraw exposed the absurdity of Bulganin's claim that we were trying to 'enslave the Arabs'.

(e) When all was over we could count our dead. This would show how few they were compared with those inflicted in Budapest by Soviet forces, and this deprived the Soviet Government of the right to apply the epithet 'barbaric' to Her Majesty's Government.

(f) The Soviet Government should know better than to suppose that Her Majesty's Government could be diverted by threats from doing what they considered right.

I added that whatever we sent ought to be endorsed by the United States, and that the President should if possible send a message to Bulganin saying so and warning him of the dangers of action on the lines hinted at in his message to the Prime Minister. Nehru (whose influence was then strong in Moscow) ought also, I thought, to be mobilized.

As I have mentioned, these telegrams were not composed in conditions of entire tranquillity. The Soviet authorities evidently thought that the ineffective demonstration of the preceding day had not been enough, and so from soon after ten o'clock onwards swarms of Russians began to arrive in front of the Embassy, carrying banners. This time they did not stay outside in the street but invaded the Embassy courtyard and garden; police guards were posted between the inner and outer front-doors to make sure they did not penetrate into the building itself. The crowd was on the whole orderly and good-tempered; they were overheard to praise the garden; when they saw anyone at a window they varied between cheerful greetings and rather unconvincing fist-shaking; they peered into the windows and climbed up the walls, pinning on to them illiterate slogans such as 'Begone away from Egypt' or 'Hands off from Egypt'. I resisted the temptation to cross 'Egypt' off these slogans and substitute 'Hungary', but I did allow myself one small joke. I had been asked to receive a delegation with protests; I refused to do this, but provided a receptacle for the protests, and quite a lot were showered into it before it was realized that it was the waste-paper basket.

Though it had its humorous side, this demonstration was not particularly agreeable, and I thought it ought to be stopped. Telephone messages to the Ministry of Foreign Affairs were of course quite ineffective. Eventually I was told that there was a General of the Militia among the crowd milling about on the snow-covered flower-beds in front of the house, so I sent one of my young men out to fetch him in. The Militia is the Soviet civil police, on the whole a rather stupid body of men and not to be confused with the secret police who, whatever they are, are not stupid. The General was in fact a very stupid-looking, red-faced man, in a grey fur hat and one of those long Russian military over-coats that almost touch the ground. I met him in the hall and he saluted me politely. I was by then getting rather angry, and said to him in a cross voice, 'How much longer is this disgraceful scene going on?' He looked at his watch, and replied, 'About another quarter of an hour.' In effect, fifteen minutes later a squad of militiamen arrived and cleared the Embassy grounds.

There were many other proofs of the synthetic nature of these demonstrations. One of the French journalists in Moscow was of Russian émigré origin and could be mistaken for a Soviet citizen. He told us afterwards that he had arrived at the similar demonstrations outside the French Embassy and said to a Russian in the crowd, 'I'm late, what's going on here?' The Russian replied, 'Things must be very badly organized in your factory. We were issued with our banners and got our instructions at nine, and the factory transport was all ready to bring us here.' I found these artificial demonstrations rather repellent, and Iris recorded in her diary that 'there was something nauseating about the Sunday School treat attitude of the demonstrators, mostly young and mostly we supposed factory workers who were in fact pawns in the Government's game of distracting attention from Hungary.'

All this nonsense was of course a considerable distraction from our serious work, and we were even afraid at one time that the demonstrators clambering about on the Embassy roofs might interfere with the aerials of our diplomatic wireless installations and so disrupt our communications with London. However this did not happen, and we were able that evening to receive the Prime Minister's instructions for his reply to Bulganin, which followed the general lines of my suggestions. The next day, being November 7th, the crowds were pouring along the road past the Embassy on their way to and from the Red Square celebrations. The gates of the Embassy were open and the guards had not been increased, but there was not the slightest sign of hostility. We found the late events a welcome reason not to attend the parade on the Red Square or the Kremlin party, and indeed mostly stayed peacefully at home. On the evening of November 9th, however, we went to a concert to hear Richter playing Prokoviev and Shostakovich; the concert audiences were always the most civilized in Moscow, and the whole evening, as Iris recorded, restored our faith in Russians a little.

But though we felt better about the ordinary Russians we still thought it wiser to avoid the leaders. I had been, until then, on a footing of at any rate ostensible cordiality with them, and I felt it was impossible to resume this after all that had happened in Hungary and after the rocket-rattling and the staged demonstrations against our Embassy. However Gomulka came on an official visit to Moscow in the middle of the month, and the Western Ambassadors, who had all since Hungary kept away from all Soviet receptions, thought that in courtesy to the new Polish Prime Minister we ought to go to the functions given in his honour. We subsequently regretted this. At the Kremlin reception Khrushchev made a furious speech saying that the

British and French Governments had been behaving like bandits. My private opinion was that this was not far from the truth, but I also thought that it came badly from Khrushchev, whose hands were still dripping with Hungarian blood, and that in any case he had no business to say it at a party to which he had invited the British and French Ambassadors. Accordingly I told the French Ambassador that I thought we ought to walk out. Dejean, who knew no Russian, had not heard what was said, and in any case he was always in favour of what he called 'playing the diplomatic game'. However I persuaded him to agree. Before we left I told Chip Bohlen what we were doing, and as Dejean and I stalked out I was touched and grateful to see that Bohlen had rounded up all the other N.A.T.O. Ambassadors (all anti-Suez to a man) like a sheep-dog with a flock of sheep, and brought them out behind us. We all had to march out again next day at the Polish Embassy reception for Gomulka, when Khrushchev, sounding drunk as Iris's diary records, made his notorious 'We shall bury you' speech.

Bohlen's attitude throughout all this period was beyond praise. Though in private savagely critical of our Suez policy he maintained the most complete solidarity in public. I had some difficulty in dissuading him from driving round to our Embassy with his flag flying during the November 6th demonstration against us, and I had reason to believe that he was warning the Russians privately not to interpret American anger with us over Suez as a licence to Russia to attack us.

When it was all over I attempted, in a long despatch to the Foreign Office, to analyse the relationship between Hungary and Suez. Soviet operations in Hungary, I pointed out, had been in two phases, from October 24th to 30th when their troops were in action in response to an invitation by the then Hungarian Government to intervene to restore order, and from November 3rd and 4th onwards when they were on their own after overthrowing Nagy. The first action was inevitable; the Soviet Government was certain to respond to any such invitation. The question was whether the second would have occurred anyway or was influenced by the Anglo-French intervention in Egypt which occurred between the two phases.

The first phase ended with the withdrawal of Soviet troops from Budapest on October 30th. When Zhukov, then Minister of Defence, told the American Ambassador that this withdrawal had been ordered he looked very ill-tempered and said, 'let them [the Hungarians] get on with it as best they can', making as he said this the famous Russian dismissive gesture of the hand. Mikoyan and Suslov were then in, or just back from, Budapest. Mikoyan probably wanted Nagy to be built up as a Gomulka. Suslov probably wanted firm action, and the Army would have supported this. It looked from what Zhukov had said to Bohlen on October 30th as if the strong-arm party had been over-ruled, and the declaration of 'Dominion Status' for the satellites issued that day carried the same suggestion. This declaration might have been intended as a deception to lull the Hungarians till reinforcements arrived, but I thought this unlikely; Zhukov had said on October 30th that there were enough Soviet troops in Hungary to finish the job, and it would surely have been easier to carry on than to announce withdrawal, thus cancelling the invitation received from the Hungarian Government. It thus looked to me as if a real decision to withdraw from Budapest was taken on October 29th or 30th.

Then two things happened. The first was the Anglo-French ultimatum announced in the House of Commons on October 30th. The second was that Nagy failed to do what Mikoyan expected of him, asked for the withdrawal of Soviet troops from all of Hungary, proclaimed Hungarian neutrality and announced her withdrawal from the Warsaw Pact.

This placed the Soviet Government in a quandary. The second development clearly strengthened the firm-hand party. But the Soviet Government's moral stand about Egypt would be weakened if they were simultaneously suppressing Hungary. Perhaps, I suggested, Khrushchev and Mikoyan might have wished to hold off in Hungary, their general position being to freeze Europe while building up in the Middle East and Asia. But Nagy's extreme policy made it impossible for them to do so.

The strong-arm party could now use three arguments, it seemed to me, deriving from the Suez situation. First, the Anglo-French action would alienate the Asia countries from the West and so weaken Asian opposition to the Soviet Union over Hungary. Secondly, the British and French had taken the law into their own hands in Egypt and were getting away with it, as it seemed at that moment, so why should Russia not do so in what had been her own preserve? Thirdly, the Soviet Government could not do much for Egypt and could not take two simultaneous defeats, Egypt and Hungary. My conclusion was that these arguments had prevailed and that the strong-arm party had won. But the Soviet decision to go all out in Hungary was caused by Nagy and not by Suez, though the latter had contributed something.

Reverting briefly to this point again in the last quarterly report I sent from Moscow, at the end of December 1956, I enumerated the difficulties the Soviet Government had been facing. They had had troubles with Yugoslavia and with Poland. There had been strikes in Moscow factories and student troubles at Moscow University. Finally there was the catastrophe in Hungary. In this respect Suez had been a God-send to them. Both Suez and Hungary were the consequences of actions taken by the Soviet Government. But they were undesired and unforeseen consequences, inspired by the unpredictable reactions of others to Soviet actions designed to produce different results, and they caused the Soviet Government to adopt courses which they did not intend to follow and which vitiated their own previous policies. In Hungary the policy of cautious relaxation of pressure had led to an explosion. In the Middle East Soviet sapping and mining at Western positions, while outwardly professing to respect them, caused the Western Powers to react with unexpected violence, and the Soviet Government in order to maintain its prestige with the Arabs threatened Great Britain and France with force and thus destroyed their own policy of *détente* with the West.

That Suez had, nevertheless, still been a God-send to Russia was clear to me from a little incident in my own experience. After the Hungarian Revolution had started, but before the Anglo-French ultimatum, I had received the first call of a newly-arrived Asian Ambassador. He asked me what I thought of events in Budapest. I said it was not for me to comment, but I thought he and his fellow-Asians ought to study what was happening in

Hungary closely if they wished to understand the real nature of Communism. He agreed, and said he thought Hungary would be a lesson to them all. A few days later he and his country were in full cry against British imperialism in Egypt, and the lesson of Hungary was lost. Russia had been let off the hook.

The time for my own departure from Moscow was now approaching. When I had been on leave the previous summer I had been told that I was to come back to the Foreign Office in January 1957 to succeed Harold Caccia as the Deputy Under-Secretary (Political). But during the Suez crisis I began to wonder if I should ever take up this post. I drafted several letters of resignation from the Service, but in the end sent none of them off.

The question whether and in what circumstances Civil Servants should resign on policy questions is a difficult one. Civil Servants are there to carry out the orders of their political masters. If they disagree with these orders they can say so and try to get them changed. But in the last resort they must carry out Ministers' orders even if they do disagree with them; if they were to resign every time they disagreed, orderly administration would become impossible. Of course cases may arise in which Civil Servants consider that the orders given to them are deeply repugnant to their consciences or fatally prejudicial to the national interests, and in these circumstances they have no option but to resign, though even so they should probably do this in such a way as to cause the least possible embarrassment to the Government.

In the case of Suez I was not being given any orders (I should have found things much more difficult if I had been the British representative at the United Nations) and I could tell myself that my resignation at that juncture, however discreetly managed, would have given the Russians a propaganda advantage which they had done nothing to earn. I hope that in reaching this con-clusion I was not rationalizing a reluctance to abandon a career to which I was devoted and on which my livelihood and that of my family depended. But when, eighteen months later, I did decide to leave the Diplomatic Service my experiences at the time of Suez were not without their weight.

In my final Quarterly Report, from which I have already quoted, I observed that my impending departure from Moscow, which I had visualized on my return from leave in October as likely to take place in circumstances of at least outward good-will, was now approaching amid an atmosphere of mutual re-criminations and social boycott, for me a somewhat melancholy conclusion to a period which had earlier seemed likely to coincide with relatively friendly Anglo-Soviet relations. At the diplomatic functions we had attended since the crisis I had avoided all contact with the Soviet leaders until, at a Burmese Embassy reception on January 4th, I found myself unable to avoid shaking hands with Bulganin and Shepilov. Bulganin behaved with dignity, merely nodding and passing on. Shepilov, brash and tactless as usual, cornered the American Ambassador and myself and asked us why we had been failing to turn up at Russian official receptions; we took some pleasure in telling him that this was because of events in Hungary and because of the offensive speeches liable to be made at such parties, which led to incidents we should prefer to avoid. Shepilov asked me a little nervously if I would accept an invitation to a farewell lunch. I said I would, and a stiff and dismal occasion it was, but I left on January 14th without having asked to pay farewell calls on Bulganin and Khrushchev.

SEVEN

An Early Resignation

My time as Ambassador in Moscow, disagreeable though its ending had proved to be, was the most satisfactory part of my diplomatic career. I felt I was playing in the top league. I was seeing as much as I wanted of the leaders of one of the world's two greatest Powers. If I went on leave to England I regularly saw the Prime Minister and the Foreign Secretary. If I took a holiday in Persia the Shah would summon me from Isfahan for a long private interview. The numerous Heads of State who visited Moscow in my time always had a talk with me.

When I returned to London in January 1957 to become the Deputy Under-Secretary (Political), the second official, as opposed to Ministerial, position in the Foreign Office, the same high-level situation prevailed, though my standard of living declined sharply from Rolls-Royce and chauffeur to standing in bus queues. I started by supervising only the Northern and Southern Departments, but I soon found that this did not give me enough to do and managed in due course to take over the Middle East Departments as well. These departments all involved crises of various kinds, and Iris's diary for the period is full of entries like 'W. constantly telephoning to Selwyn Lloyd and Macmillan, Cyprus and Lebanon are both being tiresome.' This was the period when, under the astute guidance of Mr. Harold Macmillan, England was making a surprising recovery from the humiliating disaster of Suez. The 'special relationship' with America was artificially revived for the last time, largely owing to the Prime Minister's personal ties with President Eisenhower. Even in the Middle East the British position, with American support, seemed to be recovering, though this was in fact only a pause in its inevitable decline. N.A.T.O. was fairly solid, and the first tentative steps

6

towards Europe were being made. When de Gaulle returned to power in the spring of 1958 good relations with him too seemed to have been established. Behind all this confident façade a surreptitious dismantling of our remaining Empire was proceeding; the Macmillan Government was walking backwards out of Africa. With all of this, except the African operation, I was closely concerned.

This involved a lot of travelling. In May 1957 I attended a N.A.T.O. meeting in Bonn. In September of the same year I went with Selwyn Lloyd on an official visit to Belgrade. We lunched with Tito in the White Palace, and had a rowdy evening with Koca Popovic, then Yugoslav Foreign Minister. Selwyn Lloyd was in his most bullying mood, and made his embarrassed and largely Wykehamical staff sing silly songs. Next month I went off with him and Macmillan to Washington. There were long and friendly meetings with Eisenhower in the White House, and Vice-President Nixon, lunching at the British Embassy, held forth impeccably, but not entirely convincingly, about the special relationship, America's most reliable ally, and so forth; the Prime Minister's reaction to this was to fall asleep.

In January I went with Selwyn Lloyd to Ankara for a meeting of the Council of the Baghdad Pact. It was during this meeting that I revised my opinion of him. It had not been easy to take him seriously as Foreign Secretary when Eden was Prime Minister, since at that time all foreign policy was run from No. 10, and when I returned to the Foreign Office I found, in daily contact with Selwyn Lloyd, that his teasing, leg-pulling, bullying manner was not sympathetic. But living with him for some days at close quarters in the Ankara Embassy I suddenly realized that I liked and even respected him and that he was really a very able Minister.

By the time of that meeting he had re-established very close relations with John Foster Dulles, who was also in Ankara. Indeed I wondered at times if they were not almost too close; they had long conversations in corners which I often suspected had nothing to do with matters on the agenda. Dulles was a man whom it was impossible to like or even trust, but he was an efficient operator. He was always ready with an authoritative, well thought-out answer to the trickiest question; he would open and shut his mouth, silently, once or twice, and then out would come a neat, ingenious and not always evasive reply. The other notable figure of the conference was the Turkish Prime Minister, Adnam Menderes, who looked like a large, sleek, powerful cat; his political enemies had him hanged a few years later.

When the meeting was over I went off on a tour of the Middle East, an area in whose affairs I was by now deeply concerned but which I had never in fact seen. This was for me, an inveterate sight-seer, a tantalizing journey; I visited the Lebanon without seeing Baalbek and Jordan without seeing Petra (though the King kindly offered to send me there in his aircraft). Egypt and Syria were then not in diplomatic relations with us, so I could not visit either of them. I did get a glimpse of Jerusalem, but had little time for sightseeing there. However I had an interesting interview with the Arab Governor, who had been successively a Turkish, a British and a Jordanian official and who most resembled the best type of British colonial administrator. He complained of his difficulties with the Christian sects in Jerusalem, talking of them as a British Colonial Governor might have talked unenlightened, rather childish pagans. 'There was a fight at the Holy Sepulchre only yesterday,' he said, 'between the Latins and the Greeks. If I could have got there in time all would have been well, but unfortunately I was delayed, and by the time I arrived they were hitting each other with their crosses and there was blood on the steps.' Only the Anglicans, he said, gave no trouble.

Certainly this official tour, if weak on sightseeing, was full of political interest. Politically the key area was then Iraq. The Hashemite-Nuri régime was in power, outwardly at least stable. I stayed with Michael and Esther Wright in the almost viceregal splendour of the British Embassy. It all looked secure enough, though one day, walking in the garden, Esther pointed out to me a motor-boat moored nearby in the Tigris; 'that's for our getaway'. The Embassy arranged for me to see some of the opposition to the régime; they were full of complaints, but seemed ineffective. I called on the King, Prince Abdulillah his uncle and former regent, and Nuri Pasha the Prime Minister. The King, a

rather touching young man, the walls of his simple office hung
with water-colours of Harrow, appeared to be under the influence
of his faintly sinister uncle. Nuri, the Prime Minister, was the
most powerful character of them all. I was waiting one day for a
plane in the V.I.P. lounge at Baghdad airport. The King was due
to leave for Amman, and most of the Iraqi Government except
the Prime Minister were there, chatting gaily away. Suddenly
there was a whisper, 'The Pasha, the Pasha', and Nuri appeared
in the doorway, a squat, formidable figure. A dead silence fell, as
if the headmaster had entered a classroom of noisy schoolboys.
Nuri glared at them for a moment and turned away; there was an
audible sigh of relief. A few months later the King, Abdulillah
and Nuri were all assassinated, and the British Embassy was burnt
to the ground. The appearance of stability had indeed been only
an appearance. Instability is the chronic condition of Iraq.

From Iraq I went on to the Persian Gulf. This was then, apart
from Hong Kong, the last remnant of the British Empire in Asia.
Kuwait, its brightest jewel, did not glitter very visibly. A flat,
glum, waterless town, its fantastic oil reserves had already made
its Ruler easily the richest man in the world. I called on him in his
modest little palace, somewhat incongruously guarded by small
brown sentries in bearskins and scarlet tunics. British policy was
then to persuade him to throw in his lot with Iraq. When I put
this to him, the cautious old gentleman, better informed than we
were about the stability of Nuri's régime, expressed polite scepticism and made plain his firm intention of disregarding our
advice, in spite of his dependence on Iraq for his water supply.
Water was his chief problem, a fluid much scarcer and more
precious than oil in his rich little kingdom. His desalination plant
was then producing a tenuous supply of water at about the retail
price of a good champagne. Wasteful use of water was the local
form of conspicuous display. I lunched with one of the Ruler's
brothers, a little informal lunch of sixty; in his courtyard there
were forty taps under which his guests were encouraged to wash
their hands, and in the middle of the table were a few roses,
locally grown and watered with the cash equivalent of vintage
Veuve Clicquot. Kuwait was then an altogether rather absurd
place. There were bare-legged fishermen with Cadillacs. There

were huge schools which, owing to the ferocious climate of the
Gulf, could attract no teachers, and huge hospitals which for the
same reason lacked doctors and nurses. Little boys of twelve
drove their own large cars to school along the only three miles
of made-up road. All power was in the hands of the Ruler's
family; there were the Port Sheikh, the Customs Sheikh, the
Electricity Sheikh, the Police Sheikh, the last a rather sinister
figure with a courtyard crowded with armed ruffians. I expect it
is all very different now.

Indeed the whole Gulf was then a very peculiar place, pic-
turesque in an astonishing variety of ways but not perhaps reflecting much credit on a hundred years or so of British influence.
Take Dubai, for instance. There the wide, curving creek was
crammed with fast motor-boats which, as everyone knew, were
engaged in smuggling gold into India. But it was a very beautiful
place. On one side of the creek was the Ruler's tall palace. The
other side, quite flat, was covered with one-storey houses, above
each of which projected delightful wind-towers, tall boxes with
one open traceried side facing north to catch what little cool
breeze ever blew. I walked along the beach with the Political
Agent, Peter Tripp; he wanted, quite rightly, to discuss policy,
but I was distracted by a desire to pick up the elegant, brilliantly
coloured shells, red, yellow, pink, and purple, that we trod on
with every step. From Dubai I went out to spend a day with the
Trucial Oman Scouts, a splendid survival of Kipling's India,
tough fair young officers living rough in tents in the desert, with
fierce-looking savages for troops who looked liable to stab them
in the back at any minute.

Or take Muscat, to which I flew from Dubai over the Jebel
Akhdar, the Green Mountain, flat-topped with perpendicular
sides, held by rebels against the Sultan who might, it seemed
likely, at any minute fire a rifle at our low-flying little aircraft.
Muscat's splendidly land-locked harbour, with the sinister fins of
cruising sharks always visible close inshore, is hemmed in by high
rocks crowned by Portuguese forts. The only level piece of
ground on the water-front is occupied by two buildings, the
Sultan's arcaded palace and the British Consulate-General, a
wide-verandahed building in the style of the old Raj. I called on

the old Sultan, a stout, bearded, ruffianly figure surrounded by troops of slaves. Just inside one of the Portuguese forts was a cheerful African thief in the stocks, an unexpected sight in the twentieth century. The town was walled; fierce men walking in from the surrounding hills would hang up their sten-guns on hooks inside the town gate, as in milder climes one might leave one's umbrella in the hall. All this has no doubt changed for the better now. Still, I am glad to have seen it while it lasted.

My next expedition abroad was on the inaugural flight of a B.E.A. service to Warsaw. Then, at the end of June 1958, I went to Paris with Macmillan, paying his first call on General de Gaulle after the latter's return to power. The General was then Prime Minister, not President, and all the meetings were held in the Hôtel Matignon, the beautiful official residence of French Prime Ministers. De Gaulle, at that meeting at any rate, did not at all conform to his usual stereotype of austere arrogance; he was as easy and *coulant*, in manner if not in substance, as any politician of the Fourth Republic.

Later that summer I went twice to the United States with the Foreign Secretary, on both occasions to deal with the crisis in the Middle East which led to the despatch of American troops to the Lebanon and British troops to Jordan. The first visit, on July 16th, was to Washington to discuss the American move into Beirut and to consult with the State Department whether we should or should not do something similar in Amman. We flew by night, via New York, and when we arrived at La Guardia airport early in the morning we were met by Bob Dixon who told us that British troops were already moving into Jordan. However we went on to Washington and concerted our policy and strategy with the Americans. A special session of the United States Assembly was summoned for 12th August to deal with this situation, and to this I again accompanied Selwyn Lloyd. No doubt Special Assemblies do not show the United Nations at its best or most typical, but I was not impressed by the organization, though much more so by Hammarskjöld with whom we dined privately one evening. I had met him once before in Moscow, and was struck again by his ability to clarify situations by obfuscating them. A cloud of procedural verbiage disguised the elegant way in which he was leading up to solutions which lowered tensions and let governments off awkward hooks on which they had impaled themselves. His personality seemed composed of a kind of cold fire that made him difficult to resist or oppose. His mysterious death left a gap that has not since been seriously filled.

Of course I was not travelling all the time. We had established ourselves in a nice flat in Sloane Street, and in spite of our relatively reduced circumstances were soon entertaining as actively as usual; this was possible largely because of Iris's efficient housekeeping and powers of organization. Our social life became very intense indeed. Extracts from Iris's diary, for a fairly typical week in May 1958, show the kind of thing. It starts on a Sunday in the country:

11th Sunday. Sunny and windy. Rockingham is *so* beautiful. We went over to the Buccleuchs at Broughton a.m.—French château mainly furnished and tapestried magnificently by the Duke of Montagu, ambassador in Paris in the time of Louis XIV. David Scott and his wife appeared and there was an old aunt of the Duchess. After lunch we all drove to Lord Sandwich's at Hinchingbrooke—He lives in a hideous Victorian dower-house called the Cottage. He is 83. After tea he took us round the house which is a museum of modern art, he has got a great many Paul Mazes but also many French impressionists, mainly drawings, and even the bathroom had Barbara Hepworth drawings. He had worn his Wykehamist tie in W's honour and was most touching and charming. We drove back to London taking about two hours, the traffic could have been worse.

12th. Went to Dior's show p.m. Alethea and John Nash dined and we had a nice evening.

13th. T. went to Toynbee Hall p.m. and went to Lady Gosford and Lady Hawke's dance in Belgrave Square.

14th. Frantic day. Miss Farrer came to sew. T. went to Chelsea Art School. I shopped frantically for dinner party, rushed back and cooked lunch for Miss Farrer (W. gave lunch to Donald McLachlan). Mr. Louis set my hair at 3.15. Rushed back and went on organizing dinner party. Teresa also rushed to go to two cocktail parties. [Five friends of Teresa's] dined, nice party. We had to leave early to go to a huge white tie and decorations party at the Italian Embassy for Gronchi. T. and her party went on later to Lady Elizabeth More O'Ferrall's dance at Gloucester Lodge where we joined them. All the Royal Family, anyway most of them, were at our party and we saw lots of friends. Home exhausted at about 2.30 a.m. T. got in after 3 a.m. I wore Queen of the Night [the grand Balmain dress she'd bought in Paris seven years before, see page 86].

15th. Teresa and I were thankful to have a little time for letters, etc. I went to a reception for the wedding of the Duchess of Argyll's daughter to the Duke of Rutland at Claridges; I got there early and found the press vastly outnumbered the guests and my black coat was far too long, talked to Herwarths [the German Ambassador and his wife]. Walked back as there were no taxis about. Changed in a matter of minutes and set out, W. in white tie and decorations, for Sadlers Wells, Malik (Soviet Ambassador) had sent us tickets for the first night of the Moscow Arts Theatre. They gave the Cherry Orchard with Tarasova and Gribar as Firs, it was good but not absolutely thrilling and we had to leave before the last act. Luckily we had an office car to take us to Lancaster House as it was *pouring* with rain. We waited shivering in the hall with Selwyn Lloyd for the arrival of the Royal Family. When they came Lord Airlie presented us to the Queen Mother and we took charge of her and walked up the stairs each side of her, she wore a huge white lace and net dress and lots of emeralds, we had difficulty getting near enough to communicate without stepping on her, I did once and William miraculously didn't. Our job was to present ambassadors and anyone else we saw and knew, we got better at finding out from ushers scattered about who should be presented and knowing when to move on, if we were too long we found we were stepping backwards on to Princess Margaret, and if too short forward on to the Queen and Prince Philip. The Queen Mother talked charmingly and her theme was that countries must come together. We saw the Royal Family into the supper-room and left them there. I then talked to Humphrey Mynors and his wife which was lovely after so long and to various friends. We waited 3/4 hr in cold hall for our car and got in at 1.30 a.m.

16th. Peggy Gault, Mavis Coullson and Nuby Walmisley lunched. W. is very busy owing to crises in Algeria (the army have taken control, de Gaulle's attitude is uncertain and the 4th Republic appears to be threatened) and in the Lebanon (pro-Nasser rioting in Beirut and elsewhere) and only just got back to change and go to the Three Sisters with the Herwarths. Most wonderful magic performance, essence of Chekhov and Russia and very moving, the actors as well as the audience were in tears at the final curtain. We had supper with the Herwarths, Brewster and Ellen Morris and Firebraces there too. Home at 12.30, better than last two nights. Isaiah and Aline were at the theatre, and David Cecil and other dons.

17th. W. got back after 2 p.m. owing to his crises. We looked at plans of the Warden's lodgings after lunch and decided we could arrange a good new labour-saving plan eliminating top and bottom floors.

Sunday 18th. T. slept, W. worked (very bad week-end crises in Algeria and Lebanon). I went to church. W. and I lunched with the Gascoignes. W. worked again at 4 p.m. W. and I went to an Oistrakh concert (Beethoven's violin concerto) in box with Malik and Selwyn Lloyd and Colonel (*sic*) Heath (chief whip), very enjoyable.

And so on. Almost any other week at this sort of time, selected at random, would show the same kind of thing. It will be evident from this extract that besides our own hectic London activities two other things were happening. One was that we were giving Teresa a London season, which culminated in a dance we gave for her at the Mercers' Hall the following October. This was an expensive affair, and we now think of it as the most ridiculous waste of money in which we ever involved ourselves. The other was that I was by now withdrawing from the Diplomatic Service in the direction of New College.

This had in fact been going on for some time. It all began at a dinner I attended at All Souls in May 1957, a few months after my return from Moscow, in the course of which I casually observed that I couldn't imagine anyone who had the choice of being an ambassador or the head of an Oxford college choosing to be an ambassador, adding that if I were to be offered simultaneously the Wardenship of New College and the Embassy in Washington I should of course choose New College. This was one of those light-hearted remarks one sometimes makes, largely to please one's audience, without perhaps really meaning them or at least without having thought about them properly, but it changed my whole life. I was asked, did I mean this seriously, and was I aware that the Warden of New College was about to retire and that the Fellows were looking for an outside appointment? I said no of course not, I'd no idea Alic Smith was about to give up and was just chattering. However I was asked if I would allow my name to be mentioned in New College (no Fellow of the College was at the dinner) and said I could see no harm in this.

The more I thought about this idea, the more it attracted me, but I did not at this stage take it very seriously. Clearly, however, someone in New College was taking it seriously, since I was twice asked to dine there and two Fellows of the College lunched with us in London and interrogated me quite severely. David Cecil, who was managing all this inside the College, kept asking me anxiously if I should not find life in Oxford very narrow, petty and provincial after the kind of life I had been living in London. I told him I was sure I should not (nor have I), but I was still uncertain whether I really wanted it until one day Isaiah Berlin, who was deeply involved in the whole affair, rang me up and told me I was not going to be elected. I realized from the pang I then felt that in fact I did want it very much, but I put it out of my mind from then on. Finally on April 24th, 1958, Isaiah, first with the news as usual, rang up and told me the Wardenship was going to be offered me. 'Now I suppose I shall have to make up my mind if I'm going to accept,' I said. 'It's far too late for that now,' said Isaiah, 'you're committed.'

Of course I wasn't, actually, but I very soon made up my mind that I was going to accept, and when the Bursar of New College telephoned me a few hours later I said yes at once. My reasons for accepting were basically negative rather than positive. There was first of all my future in diplomacy. Previous holders of the post I was now occupying in the Foreign Office had all gone on to become Ambassador in Washington or Paris, or Permanent

Under-Secretary. But none of these posts, for various reasons, was very likely to come my way. Washington is always a gamble, political appointments there being common. Paris, I was pretty sure, had already been promised to Bob Dixon. Harold Caccia, who was fairly certain to be the next Permanent Under-Secretary, was only a year older than me. So these doors were closed. I could go on for a year or two where I was, but then what? Agreeable posts like Madrid or Rome would seem pretty tame after Moscow. I did not fancy the United Nations after my recent experience there, and neither of us liked the idea of Bonn. I might ask to go back to Moscow, but it is often a mistake to repeat an experience that has gone well the first time. Peking seemed unlikely to become a real Embassy (nor did it in time for me to have held it) and New Delhi, though attractive, was off my beat. So my future in the Service was unclear. Moreover there was the advantage that the retiring age for Heads of Houses is seventy, whereas that for Ambassadors is sixty. And I thought that it would be nice to settle down for a bit (though in fact we have travelled almost more since I came to New College than before) and that it would be a relatively peaceful life for Iris (this proved to be an illusion). Also we were beginning to find life in London pretty intolerable. This put an end to a difference between us. I had always thought it would be nice, when we retired, to settle in London, whereas Iris had always wanted to live finally in the country. I thought our five years in St. Leonard's Terrace just after the war were not a fair test of London life, since they were years of food rationing, fuel shortages and other difficulties. But here we were, as comfortably installed as we were ever likely to be, with everything 'back to normal', and it was fairly unbearable. London was noisy, expensive and crowded, one couldn't get into it or out of it or move about in it with any comfort, and I was converted to Iris's preference for the country, eventually, with Oxford as an intervening stage.

There was, however, one more fundamental reason which pushed me in the same direction. In the earlier stages of my career I had been dealing with, and taking orders from, other diplomats, people whose mentality and outlook resembled my own and who had the same general objectives, primarily foreign policy objectives,

in mind. But in the position I had now reached I was dealing
all the time with politicians. As I have said, I liked and respected
most of the Ministers with whom I had to work. But their priorities were different from mine, their minds worked in different
ways. I found this less comfortable. At the time of Suez it had
nearly driven me to resignation. The memory of that experience
was with me as I considered my decision a year and a half later,
and it played its part in pushing me towards Oxford. In diplomacy
you are always under someone's orders, and when you are near
the top the orders come from people whose ways of thinking are
not yours. In Oxford, I realized, I should be under no one's orders.

My reasons, however, were all of them more reasons for leaving
diplomacy than for going to Oxford. In fact I had no idea what
Heads of Houses were supposed to do, and had to go and lunch
with Tom Boase, then President of Magdalen, to find out. I was
not even sure there was not an obligation to teach, for which I
felt myself wholly unqualified, and was much relieved to find
that there was not. I visualized us living in a beautiful house (and
in fact the long, shadowy vistas of the romantically beautiful
Warden's Lodgings at New College were one of the attractions
of the position) entertaining in an agreeable manner, inviting our
London and foreign friends down from time to time and getting
undergraduates in to meet them. But what else did Heads of
Houses do? I had no idea, but no doubt I should discover this as
I went along.

Meanwhile I was winding up my affairs at the Foreign Office,
which I left finally at the beginning of September 1958. I left it
with some pangs, and have often had occasion since to reflect on
the profession in which I spent twenty-eight years, the first half
of my double life. When I was appointed as Ambassador to
Moscow the *Evening Standard* published an article, illustrated
with photographs of myself and of one of my colleagues, entitled
'These Diplomatic Knights are Back Numbers'. I have not kept
a copy of this article, but I think I could reconstruct it from
memory. It said, I have little doubt, that Ambassadors used to be
important persons, deciding the fate of nations and the issues of
peace or war. Now, they were mere office-boys, on the end of a
telephone, handling only second-rate questions; all really im-

portant international matters were treated directly between Heads of State.

This type of thinking, common enough in the popular Press, rests in fact on a double fallacy. It exaggerates both the power of diplomats in the past and their present impotence. At no time in history have Ambassadors really decided policy. The illusion that they once did derives perhaps, as far as this country is concerned, from the stories, or legends, about Lord Stratford de Redcliffe, the Great Elchi. Of him one of my predecessors as Warden of New College, H. A. L. Fisher, who seems to have shared some of the illusions I have just mentioned, wrote in his *History of Europe*:

'The conditions have now passed away in which it is possible for an ambassador to involve his country in war. Telephone and telegraph make him the submissive instrument of Cabinet policy; but in 1853, the telegraph being imperfectly developed, a strong ambassador . . . could . . . take a line of his own and commit his country . . . It was long believed that Stratford de Redcliffe was the real author of the Crimean War.'

Fisher himself admits that 'the despatches of the famous ambassador do not bear out this contention'. No doubt Stratford de Redcliffe's strong personality and views, and his knowledge that these views coincided with those of Palmerston and public opinion at home, enabled him to play an unusually powerful role in Constantinople at that particular historical moment, and the fact that he had at his disposal a decisive military weapon, the British Mediterranean Fleet, put him in a position which must be nearly unique in diplomatic history.

It is clear, then, that Lord Stratford de Redcliffe's was a special case, unlikely to repeat itself with any frequency. Indeed it is difficult to think of any parallel, if it is not the much more recent one of Lord Killearn, as British Ambassador in Cairo during the Second World War, using a tank to break down the gates of King Farouk's palace when that monarch had refused to receive him. But here again it was a case of a weapon of war being handy and usable, in war-time conditions which were unique and are unlikely to recur. Perhaps an American Ambassador in South-East Asia, or a Soviet Ambassador in Eastern Europe, might find himself tempted, and able, to use a similar technique; but these would be instances more of imperialism than of diplomacy. An Ambassador behaving in this way is behaving, not as the representative of one sovereign power dealing with another sovereign power, but as the agent of a stronger power imposing its will upon a weaker and subjected, or occupied, country. It is not, in the proper sense, a diplomatic relationship at all.

Even in these very exceptional cases the Ambassador is always acting as an agent, not a principal. He is using the means at his disposal to carry out a policy decided upon somewhere else, by someone else, by, in fact, the Government of which he is an agent. For this is the essential quality of a diplomat, that he is always an agent, never a principal, that he is, as Fisher put it, the instrument of Cabinet policy not the motive power. Here we come to the second of the two popular fallacies, that this particular tool is obsolete. Quantitatively, this seems unlikely. Obsolete tools are not widely sold. But there are now more diplomats in the world than there have ever been in history. Embassies are larger, and there are more of them. Part of this may be due to mere bureaucratic inflation, one of the most widespread of modern plagues. But part must be due to a real need. When a new State emerges, one of the first things it does, perhaps even before it has a constitution, a judiciary, a police force or a functioning economy, is to appoint as many Embassies as it can afford, and sometimes more. 'Jobs for the boys' cannot alone account for this. There must be something for the boys to do, and there is.

The range of diplomatic activities is indeed very wide, much wider than it has ever been in the past. The classical activity of past Ambassadors directed itself towards a sovereign and his ministers. He negotiated with them, he tried to persuade them to follow courses acceptable to his own Government, and he kept that Government informed of their views. He is still largely confined to activities of this kind in some countries, particularly in Communist countries if he represents a non-Communist Power there. But in most other countries his range is much wider. This is because the sovereign power is, almost everywhere, much more dispersed than it used to be. Of course there is still, in every country however democratically governed, what Sir David Kelly described as 'the ruling few'. These are the political élite, the limited number of people who, however selected, carry on the actual business of government, exercise at any given moment the actual political power in a State. It is still to these that an Ambassador will wish to devote most of his attention and on whom he will principally concentrate. But in most States this élite itself has to consider the desires, the prejudices, even the moods of a much wider circle of persons, in very democratic countries the whole adult population and even in the most autocratic a circle, of varying radius, of influential persons not directly in control of government but having to be convinced or conciliated by those who are in control of government. These people, too, cannot be neglected by a modern Ambassador in so far as he has any access to them (which in Communist countries is not very far). He has to try, so far as his resources permit and the habits of the country allow, to make his own country's presence felt among them, to explain its policies to them, to engage their sympathies for it.

It is this widened range of activity that accounts in part for the immense increase of diplomatic staffs in recent years. When an ambassador had only to deal with the sovereign and his ministers he could do most of the work himself, with a little clerical and much domestic assistance. Even now he would of course be foolish to neglect the modern equivalents of sovereigns and their ministers, but this is no longer enough, and to go outside this restricted circle into the outer ranges of those who exercise, in modern States, part of the sovereign power, he needs help. Hence the numerous diplomatic staffs of most missions in these days. Hence, still more, their Press sections. For it is through the Press and the other information media, rather than directly, that an Ambassador can hope to reach and influence those outer ranges, too populous for direct personal contact to be possible with all their inhabitants.

The relations between an Embassy and the media tend to be delicate. In the bad old days before the First World War the Russian Embassy in Paris could buy and control large sections of the French Press. Such crude operations are unlikely to be possible now, at any rate in the more advanced countries, for all sorts of reasons. For one thing, important papers are now not so cheap.

But even if newspapers, or journalists, were nowadays as easy to buy as in the Paris of the Third Republic, Governments are not now likely to look with favour on purchases of national news-papers by foreign Embassies (though Communist newspapers in non-Communist countries seem to enjoy a kind of diplomatic immunity in this respect, an immunity which perhaps has to be paid for by a certain lack of authority). In general, if the Press and the media are to be influenced at all it must be by more sophis-ticated methods. They must be conciliated, not bought. They must be supplied with material they will want to use, or offered facilities of which they will wish to avail themselves. All this requires a considerable staff, considerable resources, and a high degree of patience and willingness to exert personal effort. For cultivating the media is not an end in itself. They must be culti-vated in such a way as to cause them to portray the characteristics and the policies of the cultivating diplomat's country in as favourable a light as possible. Mere hospitality to journalists will not achieve this.

Dealings with politicians and the media do not of course exhaust the functions of a modern Embassy. There are also trade promotion and the protection of the national interests and citizens abroad. These tasks were perhaps too often despised by old-fashioned diplomats, who thought of them as being more properly consular functions. Indeed I fear I must have been some-thing of an old-fashioned diplomat myself in my days in the pro-fession, since I can remember occasionally casting envious eyes on the position of Minister to the Vatican, a State with which we do not trade, which contains no resident British colony, and in which old-fashioned diplomacy can be exercised in its purest form. But such nostalgic ideas must be banished. The protection and pro-motion of trade must be among the highest priorities of any diplomat, and most of all of a British diplomat since he represents a country which must live or die by its international commerce. Indeed this high priority, top priority in fact, for trade promotion is now officially recognized by the Foreign Office, which is per-haps even over-compensating for its former neglect of this side of its work, to an extent which sometimes disconcerts some politi-cally-minded recruits who joined the Service with different expectations. They feel that what they are being asked to do may be magnificent, but it is not diplomacy. The alienation between this type of diplomatic recruit and trade promotion is indeed often mutual; in spite of their earnest application to trade statistics, their assiduous cultivation of local business contacts, this kind of young man often seems to the British exporter not exactly the type he is used to or that he can most usefully consult. One can only say that if there are failures they are due neither to lack of policy direction from the centre nor to any ill-will in the Embassies. At both the importance of the task is recognized; the difficulties arise sometimes from temperament, sometimes from the sheer difficulty of the operation, and sometimes, it must be confessed, from the insularity and inefficiency of some British exporting firms. The other side of the work traditionally regarded as consular, the protection of nationals, remains still the primary concern of the consulates or of the consular section of an Embassy. But in many countries an Ambassador will find it will take up a considerable proportion of his time; one has only to think of cases like Gerald Brooke or Timothy Davey.

If one considers all these activities, the traditional negotiating and persuading role, the Press work, the promotion of trade, the protection of nationals, it is perhaps no longer a matter for surprise that Embassy staffs are now as large as they often are. But, it will be said, these are all low-level, bureaucratic affairs. The great questions of policy are settled direct between Heads of State. Embassies, if they come into it at all, are merely post-offices through which governmental communications pass. They can have no influence on these communications; they are merely there, at the other end of the telegraph or telephone, to take orders which they must carry out without further ado. If serious difficulties arise the Heads of Government or Foreign Ministers will meet to sort them out.

Here again is a whole series of popular fallacies. One of these is that telecommunications systems work only one way. Those who argue like this forget that if an Ambassador can now receive instructions practically instantaneously, he can also communicate with his own Government by the same method, and can thus influence his instructions in a way not open to his predecessors in the days before Marconi. I can perhaps best illustrate this by a simple example from my own experience. This was the occasion when, as described on page 145, I was summoned from my Moscow bed to receive the first of Khrushchev's rocket-rattling threats, that delivered to Great Britain and France at the time of Suez. Next morning I sent to London suggestions for a possible answer, and most of these were incorporated in the instructions for a reply that I received that evening.

This episode illustrates the often neglected fact that the existence of the telegram may give an Ambassador more, not less, influence on policy, even on major policy. Before the days of telegrams, instructions to an Ambassador were drafted in the Foreign Office, necessarily on the advice of the permanent officials there and often in ignorance of the Ambassador's views. When they arrived he had little discretion; he had to act on them as they were, with any discretion they might expressly allow but no more, because to query them with his home Government would have meant an unacceptable delay. But now if an Ambassador receives instructions which he considers misconceived he generally has an opportunity to put any objection he may have telegraphically to his Government, and since his objections are those of the man on the spot, best able to judge the local implications of the action proposed, they are likely to command respect.

The extent to which an Ambassador can influence his Government must of course depend on all sorts of factors, on his personality and powers of expression for instance, and also on whether his views are likely to accord with those of his masters at home. If he is a man of strong character and can draft lucidly, if his views agree with the views held at home, he may be very influential, and not always for good. A classic example of this was Sir Nevile Henderson in Berlin just before the Second World War. He was, in his limited way, an efficient operator, and the mistaken views he sincerely held about German policy were all too welcome to his masters in London. As a result he had greater influence over them than did the officials in the Foreign Office who, in this instance, were right while he was wrong.

It is thus probably a mistake to underrate the influence of a modern Ambassador, or to suppose that modern communications have in any way diminished it. He remains, as I have said, an agent, not a principal, but he is an important and influential agent still. Nevertheless many people continue to believe that the importance of the agent is shrinking because of the frequency with which the principals now encounter one another. To believe this is to misconceive the whole nature and purpose of these encounters of principals, summit conferences, official visits and so on, and it is perhaps worth while considering this question a little further.

They are not so novel, these encounters. The Field of the Cloth of Gold, Napoleon and Alexander I on the raft at Tilsit, William II and Nicholas II in their yachts at Björkö are obvious historical examples. They are also, as it happens, rather good examples of how futile such meetings often turn out to be in the long run. They are not necessarily futile, however; indeed they can serve a very useful purpose if this purpose is clearly understood. They are a way in which the leaders of States can get to know each other's personalities, temperaments and opinions. They can improve the atmosphere between countries that have been getting at cross-purposes. They are a way of forcing heads of Governments, so often distracted by the endless pressure of current or domestic affairs, to concentrate wholly for a limited space of time on what ought to be a limited number of important questions of foreign policy. They may enable them to bring to a conclusion a protracted and complicated negotiation which has reached a point where a few clear and well-defined decisions are needed. They may also allow them to set in motion other negotiations which will subsequently continue through normal channels.

If high-level meetings are confined to objectives of this kind they may well serve a very useful purpose. But it is idle to expect them to bring about solutions of complicated questions about which the parties involved are still far apart. Nor is it sensible to try to use meetings of this kind to arrive at some general settlement of world problems of the sort that have been baffling the Governments for years, such as disarmament. The time available is always too short for such complicated negotiations, the level of discussion too general, and there is always the danger of agreement on vague and ambiguous formulae which each side afterwards interprets differently, with consequential bickering and loss of confidence.

The good and the bad sides of summit meetings are clearly visible in the contrast between the meetings of this kind held during the Second World War and since. The war-time ones had defined objectives, chiefly relating to the prosecution of the war, and they had been carefully prepared beforehand by the military and civilian staffs to the point where all that was needed was a high-level decision. The meetings were therefore very useful for this purpose. On the other hand the Potsdam Conference in 1945, and the Geneva Summit Meeting in 1955, both of which I attended, attempted to settle a number of large, general questions on which the views of the principals were very far apart. They were therefore quite ineffective, and largely a waste of time for all concerned.

There is another form of summit meeting, and that is the State or ministerial visit to a foreign capital. This is a kind of summit meeting *à deux*, and it has most of the merits and demerits of other summit meetings. These bilateral meetings come in two varieties. There is the mainly business meeting, of the type, say, of those paid to Washington by the British Prime Minister or the German Chancellor. These are primarily to discuss affairs of current importance, and in a sense their agenda might well, it could be thought, be left for transaction by the Ambassadors and the State Department. But they have the additional advantage of allowing the visitor to establish, if he can, suitable personal relations with the President; they engage the President's attention, briefly at least, on the problems and needs of the visitor's country, and at the very least they afford access to the President who is not necessarily or always available to an Ambassador.

Then there are the more full-dress State visits that Heads of State pay each other. At these some sort of business can be, and often is, transacted on the side, generally by an accompanying Foreign Minister. But the main object is different. It is to demonstrate publicly the good relations existing between the two States, or in some cases to create them where they do not exist in the public mind but where the Governments concerned wish to create them; a good example of the latter is the series of visits paid by Edward

VII to Paris at the turn of the century, which served to efface the memory of Fashoda and to pave the way for the *Entente Cordiale*. The visits which Western statesmen pay to Moscow, or which Khrushchev in his time paid to Delhi, London and Washington, tend to fall into this category, and so perhaps do President Nixon's to Peking and Moscow.

It is sometimes thought that Ambassadors resent these visits by Heads of State or of Government, as tending to diminish their own stature in their country of accreditation. I doubt if any sensible Ambassador feels this way. The visit of a leading personality from his own country almost always enables an Ambassador to enlarge his own contacts. He has to arrange continuous meetings with the visitor's opposite numbers in the capital where he resides, while the visit lasts he will see these opposite numbers more continuously than is normally possible, and if the visit has gone well it will leave behind good and closer relations with them which will be useful to him in the future. It also has the advantage of putting him in touch with members of his own Government, in a way which is not always easy for him at home. Finally he knows that when the visitor goes home it will be left to him to carry on the real day-to-day problems of the relationship between the two countries, few of which are likely to have been fundamentally altered by the visit.

This is, really, the point of diplomacy. It ensures continuity in relations between countries. High-level visits are important but spasmodic and of short duration. In between, contact must be maintained, and it is the Embassies that do this. In this continuous process the importance of social relations must not be overlooked. There is much that is futile about the social side of diplomacy, particularly in the exchange of hospitality between diplomats themselves, in the protocol calls, in the National Day receptions. Nevertheless without a high degree of social activity and entertainment much of the work of diplomacy could not get done, and those responsible for the selection of recruits for the diplomatic service should not overlook this and should realize that intelligence and integrity, indispensable as they are, are not sufficient qualifications for this career; self-confidence and social ease are also essential.

What I have so far written might suggest that the whole function of an Embassy was negotiation, under which heading one can properly include the protection of interests, the promotion of trade, Press work and social activities. But there is another and quite different function of an Embassy, and that is reporting. It is important for an Ambassador that his home Government should have a proper understanding of the developments, political and economic, in his country of accreditation. The home Government itself needs information of this kind in forming its decisions on policy towards the foreign country concerned. Its demands for information are sometimes excessive. To some hard-pressed Embassies it occasionally seems as if their controlling Ministry collects information as a stamp-collector collects stamps, not because it means to make any particular use of the information but simply in the interests of completeness. The extent to which it is the duty of an Embassy itself to supply all the information required inevitably varies from country to country. It is never possible to rely entirely on the Press for this purpose. For one thing, the interest of the Press is different; it is generally to supply the public with immediate news of daily happenings, whereas what the Embassy and its home Government need is a proper picture of long-term developments. For another, in many countries the foreign Press is scarcely represented. In others, it is denied access to much important information or is prevented by censorship from reporting it. This is of course particularly true in Communist countries, and here the reporting function of an Embassy is particularly important, and particularly difficult owing to the generally secretive nature of Communist régimes.

It is perhaps worth dwelling briefly on the nature of diplomacy in Communist countries. It is, at times, a frustrating experience. There are moments, as I have recorded, when a diplomat in Moscow wonders whether he is really earning his salary. His negotiations consist, to a great extent, in conveying messages to Soviet Ministers or officials whose almost invariable reply, even at the highest level, is 'I will consult my Government.' Negotiating in Moscow has been compared to dealing with a slot-machine. You put in your coin, and you may or may not get something out. If you do it will probably turn out to be useless. If nothing comes at once you can shake the machine, but it is useless to talk to it. The other normal diplomatic functions hardly exist. There are no commercial relations in the ordinary sense, since all trade is nationalized. Personal contacts are rare and strictly controlled. The Press is inaccessible. Reporting is baffled by the veil of secrecy hung before almost everything, including subjects that in other countries would be a matter for normal Press reports.

Faced with all this, the diplomat in Moscow often wonders why he is there. His Government's messages could, he sometimes feels, be sent through the post. His reports could be compiled at home by an intelligent reader of the Soviet Press. Commercial relations could be conducted with the Soviet Trade Delegations abroad. Such pessimism, natural though it is, is in my opinion unjustified. When I was first in Moscow, in the middle thirties, *The Times* refused to keep a correspondent in Moscow because they then maintained a principle of never having a correspondent anywhere where his messages were subject to censorship. Instead they kept a man in Riga, then the capital of the independent republic of Latvia. He was a conscientious man, with a good background knowledge of Russia, who read the Soviet Press and listened to Soviet broadcasts. Yet even I, then a callow Third Secretary at the Moscow Embassy, could see that his reports on Soviet affairs were often nonsense because he was outside the Moscow atmosphere. In Moscow, though we could not tell what would in fact happen, we could generally tell what would not happen; we could rule out certain developments as quite inconsistent with the feel of the place all round us. And this was in the days of Stalinism, with the purges beginning and the veil of secrecy far more impenetrable than it is now. In the relatively, though only relatively, open society of Moscow today there is much less difficulty in justifying the maintenance of an Embassy. For one thing, while Stalin was practically inaccessible to Ambassadors, contact with subsequent Soviet leaders has been easier. The study of their personalities is one of the most fascinating occupations available to a diplomat; and it is important to get it right since miscalculations about it could obviously have catastrophic consequences. As things are now an Ambassador in Moscow can often advise his Government that a certain course of action will not work, or that certain instructions require modifications; negotiation by post-box in these conditions is obviously insufficient. Even reporting, though the materials available to an Embassy are no more, and often less, than those available to the Ministries at home, is more sensible because it is written in the right atmosphere.

Of course Embassies are not the only places in which diplomacy occurs. It occurs also in Foreign Ministries. And it occurs in international organizations, of which the United Nations is the most important. Of the latter I have little direct experience. As I have written earlier I used to attend sessions of the League of Nations during its decline, and I have been to one or two meetings of the United Nations. But others are better qualified than I am to write of United Nations' diplomacy. To a relative outsider it seems to have the defects of its qualities. Its qualities are that it provides a machinery for settling disputes that might otherwise become more dangerous, a meeting-place for almost all the nations of the world, a channel for non-political international activity. Its defects are that the machinery sometimes becomes an end in itself, that the object of the complicated exercise sometimes seems to be to pass resolutions which, once passed, have no impact either way on the problems that are alleged to form their content, and that the channels become clogged and absorb too much energy and resources which could be more profitably deployed elsewhere. These are the inevitable defects of any international organization which is based on the sovereign equality of all States (they were just as prevalent in the League of Nations), and they do not outweigh the advantages of the organization, which, if it did not exist, would certainly have to be invented. They clearly present the diplomats involved in its operations with special problems, on which I am not qualified to pronounce.

Diplomacy in a Foreign Ministry is not often thought of in those terms, but is of course an important part of the profession. Nowadays most countries organize their diplomatic service on the basis of interchangeability between the Ministry and missions abroad. This was not always so; in this country the Foreign Office was a separate career from the Diplomatic Service up to the time of the First World War. This was obviously bad; it resulted in a

Foreign Office ignorant of foreign countries and a Diplomatic Service ignorant of its own country. Of course some diplomats turn out to be better suited than others for service at home or abroad, but generally speaking interchangeability is now the rule. The work is different. There is more office-work at home, and less social activity, at any rate for junior officials. The work tends to be less concerned with reconciling conflicting international interests (though there is plenty of this) than with reconciling international with domestic requirements. The diplomat stationed in the Ministry has often more influence on policy than the diplomat abroad, though as I have explained earlier this is not always the case. The diplomat abroad necessarily sees policy in the light of the particular country where he is stationed, and it is his duty to make his recommendations on that basis; it is the job of the diplomat in the Ministry to apply a wider angle of vision to these recommendations. He has also of course to deal with the foreign Embassies accredited to his Government, and here his work approximates closely to that of a diplomat abroad.

What, in the light of these rather random reflections, ought we to conclude about the role of the diplomat in the modern world? I think that if one examines carefully the multifarious parts that the diplomat has to play, at home, in Embassies, in international organizations, dealing with Governments and the Press and business, negotiating and reporting, one would not find it possible to take seriously the *Evening Standard*'s views that diplomats are back numbers, or the proposal of a female writer in *The Sunday Times* that they should all be brought home and hand over their jobs to foreign correspondents. Journalists have their role and diplomats have theirs; they should not be confused. Statesmen and Foreign Ministers have their role too, a separate one from that of the diplomats who carry out their orders and whose advice they may or may not take. Ministers, in theory at least and generally in practice, decide foreign policy; diplomats carry it out, and also provide the raw material on which it is based. The personal intervention of Ministers in the execution of their own policy, in diplomacy in fact, is often useful but at best spasmodic; it cannot replace the continuous operation of diplomacy by diplomats.

The undergraduates of New College do not often consult me about their future careers; they have more expert advisers for that. However quite a number of them do come to me from time to time and ask me what I think of diplomacy as a profession. I warn them of its disadvantages, the sometimes excessive pressures of social life, the hardships suffered by a diplomat's family, the difficulties of certain posts (and the difficult and disagreeable diplomatic posts are far more numerous now than when I entered the service in 1930). But I generally conclude by saying that it is an extremely rewarding occupation, providing an essential service to the nations of the world and affording the individual an opportunity to exercise most of his intellectual and moral faculties to the full. I usually add that I should not myself have left it for any position other than the one I now occupy.

Epilogue

We arrived in Oxford on October 2nd, 1958. The Lodgings were not ready, and the College had taken us rooms in a North Oxford hotel. But there had been a muddle, we were not expected, and we found ourselves in a linoleum floored, unheated attic. This was not the kind of thing to which I had recently been accustomed, and for the first (and last) time I wondered what I had let myself in for, whether I had taken the right decision.

However things straightened themselves out eventually, and by Christmas we were installed in at least part of the Lodgings. The second half of my double life had begun, and I gradually began to learn what a Head of House was supposed to do. Six years later, the University set up the Franks Commission to examine itself, and it became the fashionable pastime in Oxford to submit evidence to the Commission. I wondered whether there was anything in Oxford I knew enough about to form the basis of such a submission, and decided that all I could be said to be qualified to describe was the duties of a Head of House. However, when I had written it down it came out more like an article in the *Oxford Magazine*, so I sent it to John Vaizey, then editing that periodical, who published it on November 26th, 1964, under the heading 'Are Heads of Houses necessary?' It read as follows:

'It is alleged that when my distinguished predecessor, H. A. L. Fisher, was asked how he found the duties of Warden of New College, he replied, "They occupy me for one hour a day, and do not stretch the mind."

'When I was myself being interviewed by Fellows of the College before my election as Warden, I was told by one of them that it was a part-time job, and asked how I meant to fill the rest of my time.

'Fisher no doubt went too far, at least if his remark is applied to modern conditions. But the Fellow of New College's description of the present time-ratio deserves examination, and if it is seen to be correct his consequential question perhaps requires a generalized answer and the justification for such part-time appointments has to be made.

'What are, in fact, the present duties of a Head of House? No doubt they vary from College to College, but some generalizations are possible. He has certain largely ceremonial functions, in Chapel or in Hall, or in connexion with the College estates and livings. He presides over College meetings and over most if not all College committees. He is the ultimate authority in matters of discipline and administration. He has certain responsibilities, which vary very much as between colleges, for the admission of undergraduates. He normally takes part in the selection of new Fellows, and carries on most of the correspondence involved.

'In addition to these more or less statutory duties he generally has certain less well-defined obligations. He is expected to do a good deal of entertaining, particularly of the members of the College. If his College wishes to go in for fund-raising he will be heavily involved. He has considerable responsibility for relations with the old members of the College, who are liable to take up a good deal of his time.

'All this can be fairly time-consuming. But it seems at least doubtful whether it would constitute full-time employment for an active man or woman. Furthermore it must be observed that many, perhaps most, of the functions now performed by a Head of House could be performed, though possibly less well, by some-one else. In discipline and administration, for instance, the Head of House is only a kind of long-stop for the Dean and the Bursar respectively. Others could preside over College committees. The admission of undergratuates already occurs in some Colleges without any active participation of the Head of House. Other provisions could be made for Fellowship elections and for social and fund-raising activities.

'There is no doubt that the distribution of the functions of the Head of the House among the other members of the College would lay extra administrative burdens on the latter, who already

tend to complain of having too many, and that many of these
functions are better discharged by someone free of academic
responsibilities and able to consider the problems of the College
as a whole and to represent the College in its relations with the
rest of the University and the outside world. Still, the fact that
other, even if imperfect, solutions of the problem exist do make
it desirable to ask whether the considerable expense of maintaining part-time Heads of Houses is a proper deployment of endow-
ment income (of course no public funds are involved).

'The answer to this question is to some extent dependent on the
answer to the question put to me before my election. How do
Heads of Houses spend the rest of their time? I suspect that it is
true to say that none of the present heads of Oxford Colleges
regard their jobs as absolutely full-time. All of them have non-
College activities of one kind or another, mostly fairly considerable but occupying varying and not easily calculable proportions
of their time. Some are active in University affairs. Some are
engaged in academic or literary production (Fisher occupied
most of the remaining hours of his days as Warden of New
College in writing his *History of Europe*). Others engage in unpaid
public activities of varying kinds, membership of Royal or other
Commissions or of the University Grants Committee and similar
bodies. Others may fill up the time left vacant by their duties as
Head of House by taking on other College duties, acting as Tutor
for admissions for instance or doing some teaching.

'It remains to consider whether it is right that charitable endow-
ments should support persons devoting so considerable a proportion of their time to activities which are often extraneous to the
main purposes of the charity. In my view it is. This country has
accustomed itself for many generations to getting much of its
essential work done for nothing by men prepared to take on unpaid public work. The number of people available and suitable
for this kind of work is diminishing. In providing posts which,
while far from being sinecures, do leave their holders time for
such work, or alternatively for service to the University, or alternatively again for academic or literary production, the Colleges
are doing a public service.

'They are also doing a service to themselves. They are freeing their other members from burdens which would interfere with their primary work, and enabling certain necessary College functions to be carried out better than would otherwise be the case. They are providing themselves with appropriate representative figures for their external relations. Moreover the outside activities of Heads of Houses can often be useful to the College itself, by enlarging the College's contacts and making its name better known.

'On the whole, therefore, my conclusion would be that the institution of Head of House can be justified in present conditions. The justification depends of course on Colleges continuing to elect as their Heads persons equipped to perform one or other of the differing functions suggested for them. But this, without vanity, they will probably do.'

There is not much more to add, or at least it is too soon to add it. I have enjoyed being Warden of New College, though after fifteen years I still feel an amateur in Oxford. In the Foreign Office I had become an old pro. Good or bad, I was in my own element. In Oxford I have no share in, and no direct experience of, the two main academic activities, teaching and research. I fill in my spare time in a selection of the ways mentioned in my *Oxford Magazine* article. Iris is as busy as ever. I hope some of our activities are of some use. In a few years' time we shall be retiring to a little house we have bought in a village near Oxford, where we hope to live happily ever after.

New College. March 1973.